# The Language of Fashion

# The Language of Fashion

Roland Barthes

*Translated by Andy Stafford*

*Edited by Andy Stafford and Michael Carter*

*Oxford • New York*

This work is published with the support of the French Ministry of Culture – Centre National du Livre.

First published in France, 2004, by Editions du Seuil
© Editions du Seuil, 1993, for *Œuvres complètes – Tome 1*
© Editions du Seuil, 1994, for *Œuvres complètes – Tome 2*
© Editions du Seuil, 1995, for *Œuvres complètes – Tome 3*
and 'Preface [to the Fashion System]' (originally published by the journal *VWA* in no. 25 1998)

English edition
First published outside Australasia in 2006 by **Berg**
Editorial offices:
First Floor, Angel Court, 81 St Clements Street, Oxford OX4 1AW, UK
175 Fifth Avenue, New York, NY 10010, USA

Published in association with Power Publications, Sydney

Berg is the imprint of Oxford International Publishers Ltd.

**Library of Congress Cataloging-in-Publication Data**
Barthes, Roland.
  The language of fashion / Roland Barthes ; translated by Andy Stafford ; edited by Andy Stafford and Michael Carter.—English ed.
    p. cm.
  Includes bibliographical references and index.
  ISBN-13: 978-1-84520-380-1 (pbk.)
  ISBN-10: 1-84520-380-1 (pbk.)
  ISBN-13: 978-1-84520-379-5 (cloth)
  ISBN-10: 1-84520-379-8 (cloth)
  1. Clothing and dress—Social aspects. 2. Clothing and dress—
History. 3. Fashion—Social aspects. 4. Fashion—History. I. Stafford, Andy. II. Title.

    GT511.B363 2006
    391—dc22

                                                            2005033621

**British Library Cataloguing-in-Publication Data**
A catalogue record for this book is available from the British Library.

ISBN-13    978 1 84520 379 5 (Cloth)
           978 1 84520 380 1 (Paper)

ISBN-10    1 84520 379 8 (Cloth)
           1 84520 380 1 (Paper)

Typeset by JS Typesetting Ltd, Porthcawl, Mid Glamorgan
Printed in Great Britain by the MPG Books Group, Bodmin and King's Lynn

**www.bergpublishers.com**

# *Contents*

# *Preface*

The principal aim of this book is to bring together in one publication those writings on clothes and fashion by Roland Barthes which have yet to be translated into English. If Barthes is known for *The Fashion System* (1967, English translation 1985), his seminal if complex treatise on fashion systems and on how fashion is 'written', it is perhaps less known that he wrote also on hippies, on jewellery, and extensively on methodological problems within clothes history. It was this gap in both Barthes scholarship and in Fashion Studies that encouraged Michael Carter to ask me to translate and edit these writings. We have decided, however, not to include in this volume two of Barthes's writings on theatrical costume; we considered that his important piece on the excesses and iniquities of certain types of theatre-costume design exists already in English translation, in a slightly abridged version in Barthes's *Critical Essays* (1972 [1964]), and that, although the original version (appearing in *Théâtre Populaire* in 1955) has witty commentaries on photographs of certain costume disasters, we did not want to confuse the volume with considerations on the theatre. The same applies to Barthes's other (brief) essay on theatre costume, a 1955 review of Hélène Parmelin's *livre d'artiste* covering five twentieth-century costume designers in France. Other pieces on fashion, other than *The Fashion System* itself, are indeed available in English and are therefore not included here – mainly interviews given by Barthes around the time of the publication of *The Fashion System* – which can be found in *The Grain of the Voice. Interviews 1962–1980* (trans. Linda Coverdale, New York: Hill and Wang, 1985, 43–67).

The idea of this book, initiated by Michael Carter, was to concentrate on the key writings on clothing that predate *The Fashion*

*System,* in which Barthes tries to establish how and why people have dressed the way they do across the centuries, then to look at how Barthes moved away from clothes history towards fashion theory, and finally to set out where his analysis in *The Fashion System* went in the period immediately following. I say clothes and fashion, as this reflects a clear division in Barthes's work. For, somewhere between 1959 and 1964, a decision was made to concentrate more on contemporary (written) fashion rather than on clothes (and their history). The division of this anthology into three parts – *Clothing History, Systems and Structures, Fashion Debates and Interpretations* – reflects these shifting concerns in Barthes's research and theoretical reflections.

The pieces presented in this book appeared originally in a variety of publications in France – academic, journalistic and industry-related – of which the social history journal *Annales* is the most preponderant. From *Marie Claire* to a Catholic auxiliary nurses' publication, from *Critique* to *Communications,* Barthes's writings on clothing and fashion are clearly interdisciplinary enough to appear in a wide range of different places. They all also chart the shifts, about-turns, ruptures and spirals of Barthes's thought across the fast-paced intellectual culture of 1960s France. In twelve years, from 1957 to 1969, he goes from bemoaning the lack of decent histories of clothing to denouncing hippy ethnic fashion as a reactionary form of revolt, from using semiology to understand clothing to seeing the rhetoric of fashion as an impoverished and ultimately shallow producer of cultural forms, from considering the origins and functions of gemstones to watching a 'joust' between the rival fashion houses of Coco Chanel and André Courrèges.

This anthology has been divided into three chronological sections in order to take account of these different phases in Barthes's thought on clothing and fashion. The first part, *Clothing History,* shows Barthes in search of a solution to the thorny problem of accounting for clothing forms across history. 'History and Sociology of Clothing', published in the influential journal *Annales* in 1957, is a historical overview of hitherto existing studies on the history of clothing which discusses the weaknesses in classical, romantic, folkloric, 'archaeological', Marxist and psychological accounts of clothing forms.[1] Barthes discusses in detail the impasse of History and Structure, Change and Order, within the newly emerging dis-cipline of Cultural Studies, bemoaning the restrictive nature of the triumvirate dominating clothing explanations at the time, namely those of protection, modesty and ornamentation. This methodo-logical overview is also an early statement of Barthes's intention to use Saussure's semiology, *Annales*-inspired historical sociology and the newfangled science of structuralist linguistics, in an attempt to establish a viable history and sociology of clothing form. 'Lan-guage and Clothing', a book review for *Critique* appearing in 1959, then represents an important development in this work on clothing form in history, as Barthes slowly moves away from the ambitious programme of his earlier 'History and Sociology of Clothing' and towards the language of clothes. It contains the first hints of his interest in a sociology of contemporary fashion styles, following the realization that a history of clothing forms would require a major team of researchers, something not about to happen in late 1950s France despite the growth in sociology and the expansion of social research in this period. So Barthes sets out a clear definition of how structural linguistics and phonological analysis could be used as the basis of a sociological approach to clothing. 'Towards a Sociology of Dress', another book review, published this time in *Annales* in 1960 just as Barthes took up his research post at the VIth section of the Ecole Pratique des Hautes Etudes (EPHE) in Paris, is a comparison of the psychological works on clothing by Franz Kiener and John Carl Flügel, in which Barthes prefers the latter for its structured and fruitful insights. The former is criticized for its preference for an anthological description of the diversity of clothing forms, at the expense of a consideration of the relative signifying values inform-ing each item. Barthes thus argues, in good structuralist fashion, for a 'functional' rather than a 'substantial' description and for a struc-tural rather than an anthological approach, in which a syntactic and not a lexical study of clothes is preferred.

This first shift in Barthes's clothing theories – from substance to function – is a crucial one in defining his work through the 1960s. Part II of this anthology – *Systems and Structures* – covers the period leading up to *The Fashion System*, published with great expectations in 1967, and shows the workings behind Barthes's linguistic and structuralist 'turn'. 'Blue is in Fashion this Year', appearing in the

newly launched *Revue Française de Sociologie* in 1960, is subtitled
'A Note on Research into Signifying Units in Fashion Clothing'.
This long article is his first foray proper into fashion (as opposed
to clothing history). Building on the work in his brief essays on
women's press in *Mythologies* (1957), Barthes headed for *Elle* and
*Jardin des Modes*, to apply a semiological understanding of language
that will finally become the basis of *The Fashion System*, and in choosing the former he was looking at a hugely popular and highly
contradictory women's publication launched immediately after the
Second World War and not immune to a utopian ideology.[2] Taking
the language of fashion found in women's fashion magazines as a
signifying system, this study is the earliest version of the method
to be used in *The Fashion System*. Making eighteen general points
on fashion as a language, this article clearly anticipates the section
on 'Method' in *The Fashion System*, but there are also sections on
nominalization and generalization, on proportionality between
signifier and signified, on colour codes and on problems of taxonomy, which are eventually excluded from his *magnum opus* on
fashion systems, these either being taken as read or heavily abridged
in *The Fashion System*. The article also restricts itself to establishing a
possible classification of 'vestemes', not venturing into a systematic
inventory as in *The Fashion System*. Above all, the article is a clear,
concise and tentative explanation of structural linguistics as a possible method for understanding fashion, which serves as an excellent introduction to Barthes's later research. At the same time as
beginning to systematize fashion forms in post-war France, Barthes
reflects, in parallel and in the fine essayistic style of French writers,
on other aspects of clothing and 'meaning' in fashion forms. 'From
Gemstones to Jewellery', published in the specialist arts journal
*Jardin des Arts* in 1961, shows him at his most brilliant. The essay
is also an important statement of the role of 'detail' in fashion, a
structuralist, even proto-*post*-structuralist, analysis which sees the
tiniest detail – jewellery – as affecting the whole clothing ensemble.
Barthes also discusses how gemstones as natural minerals then
became symbols of the non-human and benefited from the poetics
of human imagination, thereby earning their paradoxical status as
items of seduction and of purity. Barthes thus performs a kind of
structural socio-psychology of the gemstone's substance and he tries

to explain its transformation, after passing through feminization, secularization and democratization, into a crucial fashion item, despite its size and non-human substance. Similarly, 'Dandyism and Fashion', published in the Franco-American cultural magazine *United States Lines Paris Review* in 1962, is both a skilful piece of literary essayism, highly provisional in its conclusions, but also a rigorously structuralist account of this masculine dressing phenomenon. It is an impressive historical survey, using sociological analysis to show how male dress in the nineteenth century gave rise to the figure of the dandy. The social need for the aristocracy to distinguish itself from the bourgeoisie led to the widespread use of the 'detail' to provide this 'distinction'. But dandy fashion was also an attempt to radically mark out the individual from the common, an early example of individuals wanting to *show* that they had thought about their clothing. Barthes then considers how modernity and democratization in fashion have served to undermine the impact of the dandy, by making radical fashion statements into a regulated market. Only women's fashion nowadays has the range – but not the social function – of the detail; fashion, concludes Barthes, has killed off dandyism.

In the wake of these 'systematizing' pieces on gemstones and dandyism, and following his research set out in '"Blue is in Fashion This Year"', Barthes drafted an early preface to *The Fashion System* (written probably in 1963 but only published posthumously in the Swiss journal [*VWA*]). As an early (first?) draft of the preface to *The Fashion System*, the piece displays significantly different emphases from the final published version of the preface. Though taken from a manuscript and very occasionally unfinished, this early preface is useful particularly given that there has been, up until now, a real gap in seeing how Barthes developed his method between 'Blue is in Fashion This Year' in 1960 and *The Fashion System* in 1967 (and a gap to which he refers in the article). The early preface is surprisingly candid, especially concerning the gains made by semiology, on the differences between the semiological and the sociological project in fashion analysis, on the importance for the study of fashion language of André Martinet's 'pertinence principle' in linguistics, and on the notion of 'totality' in clothing research. It finishes with a very frank 'autocritique' of Barthes's own project so far and the results produced, suggesting that semiology has within it the seeds of other forms of research into clothing and fashion. This second section of the book ends with three interviews, including a little-known round-table discussion with Henri Lefebvre and Jean Duvignaud, which is wide-ranging and indicative of three parallel but antagonistic critical theories of fashion.

By the time of the publication of *The Fashion System* in 1967, Barthes's name was firmly established as a major theorist of fashion in France. His theories are quoted and sought in a number of different places. The final part of this anthology, *Fashion Debates and Interpretations*, sees him deploying his essayistic skill and research results in a number of different forums. 'The Contest between Chanel and Courrèges', appearing in the women's magazine *Marie Claire* in 1967, and subtitled by the magazine 'Refereed by a Philosopher', concerns a specific 'battle' (as Barthes saw it) taking place in the French fashion industry. Though not a philosopher, Barthes shows himself a consummate essayist as he 'interprets' the meanings behind Chanel's different ranges, how little these have actually changed, how the worn and the durable in Chanel stand in opposition to the new, future-oriented offerings of Courrèges. There was thus a 'duel' taking place in French fashion of the mid-1960s, Barthes was suggesting, between classicism and modernism. The article also differentiates the conception of the body in the respective fashion houses. Finally, Barthes suggests the importance of this battle: on the same level as literature, film and music, Fashion – as a form of 'taste' – both reflects and inflects people's way of thinking and represents a form of historical and sociological 'mentality'. Then, in the wake of May 1968, the moment of intense radicalization in French student and class politics that had been slowly building since 1962, Barthes is suddenly acerbic in his criticism of hippy fashion. 'A Case of Cultural Criticism', written from Morocco in 1969 for the cultural theory journal *Communications*, is perhaps an important one for those critics (such as Rose Fortassier or Rick Rylance) who suggest that Barthes simply ignored the *parole* side of clothing in his rush to see fashion as constructed solely as a *langue*. It is a sharp (and again essayistic) 'reading' of hippy fashion and counter-cultural practice as witnessed by Barthes in Morocco, which considers hippy clothing as both deeply critical of, and compromised by, Western cultural hegemony. Without any contact with political critique, cultural critique such as that performed by hippy fashion is, he concludes, unable to escape being a kind of inverted bourgeois form. Finally, 'Showing How Rhetoric Works', published in a special number on 'Fashion and Invention' of the radical journal *Change* (and not included in Barthes's *Oeuvres complètes*), is a selection of key quotes from *The Fashion System*. It covers in particular elements of the 'rhetoric' section which are republished as fragments and edited in the light of the May 1968 events. It is a useful summary of Barthes's critique of the 'rhetoric' of fashion, but also indicative of his influence on the fashion debate following May 1968.

In the post-face to this anthology I have tried to describe in detail the about turns, dead ends and significance of Barthes's writings on clothing and fashion. Though he never wrote about what (apparently) the student of fashion would like to know about, i.e. the 'technology' of fashion forms, his work on how humans interact with clothing forms is surely useful within theories of consumption and design. All of these pieces by Roland Barthes on clothing history and fashion should be read then not simply as a complement and an aid to understanding *The Fashion System*, but as a method in preparation and as a set of writing techniques which reflect and inflect the debates and events both during a key moment in French social history *and* in today's twenty-first-century world.

## Notes

1. Interestingly Barthes starts writing on clothes and fashion history just as the idea of a museum is mooted on this subject – in the end it takes until 1991 for a clothes museum to be finished in Paris, the *Musée Galliera* (10 avenue Pierre-Ier-de-Serbie) in the 16th arrondissement of Paris.

2. See Maggie Allison, '*Elle* Magazine: From Post-war Utopias to Those of the New Millennium'. In Angela Kershaw, Pamela Moores and Hélène Stafford (eds) *The Impossible Space. Explorations of Utopia in French Writing*, Glasgow, Strathclyde Modern Language Studies vol. 6, 2004, 237–64.

# Part I

# Clothing History

# 1

# History and Sociology of Clothing

## Some Methodological Observations[1]

Up until the start of the nineteenth century there had not been, in the true sense of the word, a History of dress, but only studies in ancient archaeology or of qualitative inventories of garments.[2] At first, the History of dress was an essentially romantic notion, either providing artists, painters or men of the theatre with the necessary figurative elements of 'local colour', or enabling the historian to establish an equivalence between vestimentary form and the general mindset of the time or of the place (*Volksgeist*, Zeitgeist, spirit of the times, moral disposition, atmosphere, style, etc.). Truly scientific research on dress started in about 1860 with work by scholars and archivists such as Quicherat, Demay or Enlart,[3] or by medievalists in general. Their principal method was to treat dress as the sum of individual pieces and the garment itself as a kind of historical event, the main aim of which being above all to locate its date of birth and the circumstances surrounding it. This kind of work still dominates, to the extent that it continues to inspire the numerous vulgarized histories that abound to this day and that are linked to the development of fashion's commercial myth-making. So the History of dress is yet to benefit from the renewal of historical studies that has been taking place in France for the last thirty years: this renewal has taken account of the social and economic dimension of History, of the links between clothes and human emotional phenomena as defined by Lucien Febvre, of the demand for an ideological understanding of the past as postulated by Marxist historians. In fact, it is the whole institutional perspective on dress that is missing, a gap all the more paradoxical given that dress is both a historical and a sociological object if ever there was one.

So the inadequacies in histories of dress that we have so far are, first and foremost, those that are evident in all historicist forms of history. And yet the study of dress poses a particular epistemological problem which we would at least like to underline here: namely, that posed by the analysis of any structure as soon as it is placed in its history but is not allowed to cease being a structure. An item of clothing is indeed, at every moment of history, this balance of normative forms, all of which are constantly changing.

Histories of dress have resolved this problem, but only in a confused way. Confronted with the obligation to work on *forms*, they have tried to list *differences*: some of these are internal to the vestimentary system itself (the changes in profile), and the others, external ones, are borrowed from general history (using epoch, country, social class). There is a general weakness in these responses which is to be found both on the level of analysis and of synthesis. With regards to internal differences, no history of dress has yet bothered to take the time to define what, at any given moment, a vestimentary system might be, that is the overall axiology (constraints, prohibitions, tolerances, aberrations, fantasies, congruences and exclusions) that constitutes it. The archetypes we are given are purely graphic, that is, more aesthetic than sociological.[4] What's more, on the level of the garment itself, despite the seriousness of the inventories compiled, the analysis remains confused. On the one hand, the qualitative threshold beyond which an item changes either its form or its function is rarely stated; in other words, the very object of historical research remains ambiguous: when *does* an item of clothing *really* change, when is there *really* history?[5] On the other hand, the position of the item on the body's horizontal axis (the degrees of exteriority) is discussed only prudishly, so that the whole complex game of undergarments, garments and overgarments is never analysed in relation to their social acceptability.[6]

The attempts at external differentiation may appear more reliable, in that they are guaranteed by a general History with which we are already familiar. However, even here there is a lot missing, which is again indicative of the epistemological difficulty we mentioned earlier. Geographically speaking, histories of dress have not taken stock of the law established by folklorists in relation to folkloric facts. Any vestimentary system is either regional or international, but it is never national.[7] The geographical presentation in histories of dress is always based on a 'leadership' in fashion which is aristocratic, without this leadership ever being placed in its political nor, in this instance, European context. Socially, moreover, histories of dress rarely consider anything but royal or aristocratic outfits. Not only is social class reduced here to an 'image' (the lord, the lady, etc.), deprived of its ideological content.[8] But also, outside of the leisured classes, dress is never linked to the work experienced by the wearer: the whole problem of how clothes are functionalized is ignored. Finally, historical periodization is presented in these histories of dress in a distorting and narrow manner. The difficulties involved in any historical periodization are well known.[9] Lucien Febvre proposed that we substitute one simple, central date for the two dates at both ends; this rule would be all the more appropriate in the history of dress given that, in relation to clothes, both the start and finish of a fashion (in its general sense) always occur over a period of time. In any case, if it is possible to date the appearance of a garment to within one year by finding its circumstantial origins, it is a distortion to confuse the invention of a fashion with its adoption and even more so to assign a rigorous end-date to any garment. But it is precisely this that nearly all the histories of dress do, fascinated as most of them are by the chronological prestige of a particular reign, or even by the reign's political policies. In such a situation, the king remains magically affected by a charismatic function: he is considered, by essence, as *the* Wearer of Clothes.

These are the main gaps in the differential descriptions used by Histories of dress. But they are, after all, weaknesses that any broad view of History could make good. The more serious problem (because it is more specific) with regard to fundamental errors in all existing Histories of dress, is the methodological recklessness that confuses the internal and external criteria of differentiation. The garment is always conceived, implicitly, as the particular signifier of a general signified that is exterior to it (epoch, country, social class). But, without any indication, the historian will at one moment trace the history of the signifier, the evolution of profiles, whilst at the next moment tracing the history of the signified, of reigns and nations. Now these histories do not necessarily have the same tempo. First, because fashion can easily produce its own rhythm:[10] changes of forms have a relative independence in relation to the general history that supports them, even to the extent where fashion has only a *finite* number of archetypal forms, all of which implies, in the end, a partially cyclical history;[11] and then, because history is by definition made up of a 'social time which has a thousand high speeds and a thousand slow-downs' (F. Braudel[12]); consequently, the relations between vestimentary signifier and signified can never be determined in a simple and linear fashion.

Does it need to be pointed out that 'Psychologies' of dress, so numerous in the Anglo-Saxon world, are not very helpful in this respect? They leave entirely untouched the whole methodological difficulty of linking a history of clothes at any one moment to its sociology. The motivations behind dressing have been much discussed, notably on the phylogenic level, which, we should remember, have involved so much fruitless discussion on the origins of language. Why does Man dress up? The relative importance of the three following factors has been compared: protection, modesty, ornamentation.[13] Dwelling above all on the relationship between adornment and protection, and taking liberties with certain ethnographic observations (people living in a harsh climate such as the indigenous population of Tierra del Fuego apparently prefer to adorn rather than protect themselves with clothes), or with certain traits in child psychology (the child apparently adorns and disguises itself but does not dress itself), specialists have felt able to suggest that the motivation for adornment is by far the most important factor. People have even tried to reserve the word 'dress' for acts of protection, and 'adornment' for acts of ornamentation. It seems that all these discussions are victims of a 'psychological' illusion: defining a social fact such as clothes as the sum of a certain number of instincts, which, once identified on a strictly individual level, are then simply 'multiplied' to the group level, is precisely the problem that sociology is trying to leave behind.[14]

What should really interest the researcher, historian or sociologist, is not the passage from protection to ornamentation (an illusory shift), but the tendency of every bodily covering to insert itself into an organized, formal and normative system that is recognized by society. The first Roman soldiers to throw a wool cover over their shoulders so as to protect themselves from the rain were performing an act of pure protection. But once material, form and usage have become not so much embellished, but simply regimented by a defined social group (for example, the slaves in Gallo-Roman society around the second century), the garment has joined the system, has become dress (here the *penula*[15]) without our being able to find in this shift any trace of an aesthetic aim. It is the appropriation by society of a form, or a use, through rules of manufacture, that creates a garment, not the variations in its utilitarian or decorative quantum.[16] If a woman places a flower in her hair this remains a fact of pure and simple adornment, so long as the use (such as a bridegroom's crown) or the positioning (such as a flower over the ear in Gypsy dress) have not been dictated by a social group; as soon as this happens it becomes a part of dress.

This seems to be a primary truth. However, we have seen how studies of dress, whether historical or psychological, have never really considered this as a system, that is as a structure whose individual elements never have any value and which are signifiers only in as much as they are linked by a group of collective norms. Certainly, profiles, archetypal forms have been identified, most notably in graphic representations. But system is completely different from *gestalt*; it is essentially defined by normative links which justify, oblige, prohibit, tolerate, in a word control the arrangement of garments on a concrete wearer who is identified in their social and historical place: it is a *value*. So it is expressly on the level of the social that dress must be described, not in terms of aesthetic forms or psychological motivations but in terms of institution. The historian and the sociologist are not charged with simply studying tastes, fashions or comfort; they must list, coordinate and explain the rules of matching and usage, of what is constrained or prohibited, tolerated or allowed. They must establish not the 'images' or the traits of social mores, but the links and the values; they must accept this as the precondition for any attempt to establish the relation between dress and history, because it is precisely the normative connections that are, in the final instance, the vehicle of meaning. Dress is essentially part of the axiological order.

Doubtless what explains the difficulties our authors have in treating dress as a system is that it is not easy to follow the evolution of a structure through time, the continuous succession of balances whose elements change in unequal measure. This difficulty has been encountered at least, and in part resolved, by linguistics. Since Saussure, we know that language, like dress, is both a system and a history, an individual act and a collective institution. Language and dress are, at any moment in history, complete structures, constituted organically by a functional network of norms and forms; and the transformation or displacement of any one element can modify the whole, producing a new structure: so, inevitably, we are talking about a collection of balances in movement, of institutions in flux. Without wanting to get into the argument over structuralism here, it is impossible to deny the central problem. This is not to say that the problem can be solved identically, in both linguistics and dress history. But at least we can expect contemporary linguistics to provide the study of dress with outlines, materials and terms for reflection that have been developed over the last fifty years or so. Therefore we must quickly examine the methodological effects of Saussurian models on studies of dress.[17]

## Langue *and* Parole, *Dress and Dressing*

We know that for Saussure human language can be studied from two directions, that of *langue* and that of *parole*. *Langue* is the social institution, independent of the individual; it is a normative reserve from which the individual draws their *parole*, 'a virtual system that is actualized only in and through *parole*'. *Parole* is the individual act, 'an actualized manifestation of the function of *langage*', *langage* being a generic term for both *langue* and *parole*.[18] It seems to be extremely useful, by way of an analogy to clothing, to identify an institutional, fundamentally social, reality, which, independent of the individual, is like the systematic, normative reserve from which the individual draws their own clothing, and which, in correspondence to Saussure's *langue*, we propose to call *dress*. And then to distinguish this from a second, individual reality, the very act of 'getting dressed', in which the individual actualizes on their body the general inscription of dress, and which, corresponding to Saussure's *parole*, we will call *dressing*. Dress and dressing form then a generic whole, for which we propose to retain the word *clothing* (this is *langage* for Saussure).

We must obviously be careful about extending this analogy without due care and attention. Only the functional opposition of the two levels can have any methodological value. This was spotted in relation to dress itself by Trubetskoy, who established a parallel between the tasks of phonetics and those of vestimentary description.[19] The opposition dress/dressing furthermore can only help to reinforce a sociological standpoint: by strongly characterizing dress as an institution and separating this institution from the concrete and individual acts by which it (so to speak) realizes itself, we can research and isolate the social components of dress: age groups, genders, classes, degrees of civilization, localization. Dressing then remains an empirical fact, capable of being analysed with a phenomenological approach: the degree of scruffiness or dirtiness of a worn garment, for example, is part of dressing, it has no sociological value, except if scruffiness and dirtiness function as intentional signs (in a theatre costume for example). Conversely, a less obvious element of appearance, such as the differential mark in a garment for married and unmarried women in any society, will be part of dress and has a strong social value.

*Dressing* means the personal mode with which the wearer adopts (albeit badly) the dress that is proposed to them by their social group. It can have a morphological, psychological or circumstantial meaning, but it is not sociological.[20]

*Dress* is the proper object of sociological and historical research, and we have already underlined the importance of the notion of *vestimentary system*.[21]

Dress and dressing can appear to coincide sometimes, but it is not difficult to re-establish the distinction in each case: the broadness of the shoulders, for example. This is part of dressing when it corresponds exactly to the anatomy of the wearer; but part of dress when its dimension is prescribed by the group as part of a fashion. It is very obvious that there is a constant movement between dressing and dress, a dialectical exchange that is defined in relation to *langue* and *parole* as a veritable *praxis*.[22]

For the sociologist it is obviously the move from dressing to dress which is the most important. This passage can be seen in the broadening of a dressing object (with the express condition that this broadening can be defined as a phenomenon of adoption), or even in a technological initiative taken by a clothes manufacturer or syndicated producer. For example, the wearing of a coat over the shoulders, arms dangling, becomes part of dress as soon as: (1) a community makes it into a distinctive mark imposed on its members (for example, Brothers of the *Ecoles chrétiennes*); (2) the manufacturer provides the coats with internal straps for the arms with which to support the coat without rolling the sleeves up (English system). It must be noted that a dressing object that is at first constituted by the degrading of a dress object can subsequently transform itself once more into a secondary dress object: this occurs as soon as this degrading actually functions as a collective sign, as a value. For example, the outfit can gesture towards the using of all of the buttons on the shirt; and then a dressing object of some sort leaves the top two buttons undone: this omission becomes dress again as soon as it is constituted as a norm by a particular group (such as in dandyism).

Fashion is always part of dress; but its origins can represent either of our two categories. Fashion can be part of a dress object that has been artificially elaborated by specialists at any one moment (for example, haute couture); at another moment, it can be constructed by the propagation of a simple act of dressing that is then reproduced at the collective level and for a number of reasons.[23] This ordering of objects needs to be studied carefully. But what we can perhaps now foresee is that the link between dressing and dress is a semantic one: the meaning of a garment increases as we move from dressing to dress. Dressing is a weak form of meaning, it expresses more than it notifies; dress on the contrary is a strong form of meaning, it constitutes an intellectual, notifying relation between a wearer and their group.

## Diachrony and Synchrony

We have already pointed out that it was necessary to distinguish in clothes between the synchronic or systematic level and the diachronic or processive level. Once again as with language, the major problem here is that of putting together, in a truly dialectical snapshot, the link between system and process. George H. Darwin, nephew of Charles Darwin, got an inkling of this problem when he established a parallel between biological and vestimentary development, with the garment corresponding to an organism and the system (*a whole type of garments*) to a species.[24] In fact, the problem cannot be resolved so long as the system has not been defined according to internal criteria, something that histories of dress have not yet done. Linguistics, for its part, is in the process of working to clarify the links between synchrony and diachrony, without yet succeeding; in other words, the science of dress, which has as yet to be constituted, has so far not carefully examined the data. But by looking to the example of linguistics we are able to suggest two methodological caveats – historical and sociological – to guide us towards a definitive explanation. We must first agree to make the notion of system more flexible, that is to think of structures in terms of tendencies rather than perhaps in terms of a rigid equilibrium. Clothes live in tight symbiosis with their historical context, much more so than language; violent historical episodes (wars, exoduses, revolutions) can rapidly smash a system; but also, in contrast to language, the recasting of the system is much quicker. However, it would not be desirable, at this point, to reintroduce, into the flux of vestimentary forms, any external determinisms before having identified all of the internal factors that, within the system itself, play at least a part in its evolution.[25]

## *Signifier and Signified*

As we know, Saussure posited a science of meanings under the name of semiology, of which linguistic semantics would be but a part. It goes without saying that dress – which cannot be reduced to its protective or ornamental function – is a privileged semiological field: one could say that it is the signifying function of dress which makes it a total social object. Drawing on the observations on the sign made by Ignace Meyerson,[26] let us distinguish, for dress, between indexical objects and signifying or notifying ones:

*Indices* The index operates outside of any intention of directed behaviour. The link that many histories have established between dress and the 'spirit' of an age would be part of the indexical, if such a link could be proven to have any scientific power which is, as yet, far from being the case. We find more reliable indexical objects in studies by a certain number of Anglo-Saxon writers, where dress is treated as the index of a certain interiority. This research has taken two directions. Firstly, it has been properly psychological (in the United States), in the sense of a psychology of choices and motivations, in which attempts have been made to identify the hierarchy of motives in vestimentary choices, with the aid of question-naires and even tests.[27] But here we are really talking about a limited number of indices which the psychology in question has never tried to link to a psychic, or social, totality. The second direction in this research on the psychology of dress takes its inspiration from psychoanalysis, in the widest sense of the term. It is easy for everyone to see what a psychoanalytical reading could find in a cultural object whose erotic implications are fairly obvious and whose formal characteristics lend themselves easily to symbolic interpretations; these attempts at explaining cannot be assessed without making an overall judgement on psychoanalysis itself, which is not our job here. However, whilst remaining outside of a psychoanalytical postulate, it seems that analyses of this type are more fruitful when it comes to describing what we might call expressions of personality (*self-expression, self-bodility*, in the classifications made by Flügel[28]), than when analysing symbolization proper, where we have, it seems, to be wary of 'shortcuts'.[29] From a methodological point of view what is interesting in a psychoanalytical explanation, is that the notion of index is itself ambiguous: is vestimentary form really an index, produced outside of any intention? Within the psychoanalytical perspective there is always an (unconscious) choice of an outfit by the collective, or of a way of dressing on the part of the wearer; and here dress is always set up as an object for possible deciphering by the person reading it (group, super-Ego or analyst). Dress, for the psychoanalyst, is meaning more than index: the notion of censorship lays the basis for the notion of control in social psychology, just as the notion of sublimation is nothing other than the psychoanalytical version of the process of rationalization. It would appear then that the equivalences identified by psychoanalysis are more factors of expression than indices.

*Meanings or Notifications*   Between the indexical and the notifying, there may well be mobile and ill-defined boundaries: such and such an object of notification can come from a previous indexical object – the masculine sports-outfit (of English origin) was at first simply the index of the need for the liberation of the body; then, once detached from its function and becoming an outfit (a two-piece with tweed jacket), it signified, or notified, a need which, from then on, was less felt than accepted. Generally, the study of phenomena in vestimentary signification relies heavily on the care with which dress has been analysed as a synchronic system. This is because notifying phenomena can, and in fact must, always be defined in axiological terms: the system in itself is nothing but a form; it cannot signify anything except by recourse to extra-sociological considerations (philosophy of history or psychoanalysis). It is the degree of participation in the system (be it total submission, deviations, or aberrations) that is meaningful; the *value* of a system (that is, its *value-for-ness*) can be understood only via acceptances of, or challenges to, it.

Dress is in fact nothing more than the signifier of a single main signified, which is the manner or the degree of the wearer's participation (whether a group or individual). It goes without saying that this general signified capitalizes on a certain number of secondary concepts or signifieds, that vary according to how broad the groups are, and how formalized they are, and which are signalled through these signifieds: such and such an outfit can notify concepts of psychological or socio-psychological appearance: respectability, youthfulness, intellectuality, mourning, etc. But what is notified here, through these intermediaries, is essentially the degree of integration of the wearer in relation to the society in which they live. Violent historical facts may disrupt the rhythms of fashion, bring in new systems and modify the regime of participation, but in no way do they explain the new forms. Mourning clothes may have been white once, nowadays they are black; the symbolism of colours may have a historical interest; but the social dimension refers not to the colour of mourning but to the manner of participation implied by it. Here we can see the structuralist distinction between phonetics and phonology.

History may be interested by the evolution in funereal colours; but sociology, like phonology, is interested essentially in values of opposition, of the socially meaningful.[30] Dress is, in the fullest sense, a 'social model', a more or less standardized picture of expected collective behaviour; and it is essentially at this level that it has meaning.

In any case, the notion of vestimentary signified must be studied with great care. As Mr Meyerson has emphasized, it is a limit; in reality, we are talking about 'complexes of meaning', whose equivalence can be almost entirely free. An article of clothing may seem to be 'meaningless' in itself; so we must then, more than ever, get at its social and global function, and above all at its history; because the manner in which vestimentary values are presented (forms, colours, tailoring, etc.) can very well depend on an internal history of the system. Forms may very well follow general history in a free counterpoint. Certain forms may be only the 'products', the terms of an intrinsic evolution, and not at all 'signs'; and there may be a historical arbitrariness and a certain meaningless in a garment, a 'degree zero', as the structuralists say, of vestimentary signs.

We cannot stress too much, by a way of conclusion, that the history of dress has a general epistemological value. It actually suggests to the researcher the essential problems in all cultural analysis, culture being both system and process, institution and individual act, a reserve of expression and a signifying order. In this way, it is obviously dependent not only on the other human sciences around it but also on the epistemological stage that the social sciences in general have reached. Born at the same time as the science of history, the science of dress has long lagged behind its development and now is faced with the same difficulties; the only difference is that, of all of the types of cultural research, it has, up to now, been the most overlooked, abandoned above all to rather anecdotal banalities. The history of dress bears witness in its own way to the contradiction in any science of culture: every cultural fact is both a product of history and a resistance to history. The garment, for example, is at every moment a moving equilibrium, both produced and undermined by determinisms of nature, function and amplitude, some internal, others external to the system itself. The study of dress must retain continually the plurality of these determinisms. The central methodological warning is still never to postulate too hastily a direct equivalence between the superstructure (dress) and the infrastructure (history). Contemporary epistemology understands more and more that we need to study historico-social totality as a collection of links and functions. We believe that for clothes (as for language) these stages and functions are of an axiological nature; they are the *values* that bear witness to the creative power of society over itself.

## Notes

1. Published in *Annales* 3 (July–Sept.) 1957, 430–41; *Oeuvres complètes* vol. 1, 741–51

2. A list of these investigations (by century) can be found in René Colas, *Bibliographie générale du costume et de la mode*, Paris, Librairie Colas, 1932–1933, 2 vol. (t. 11, p. 1412) and in Camille Enlart, *Manuel d'archéologie française*, Paris, Picard, 1916 (t. III ['Le costume'], pp. xxi–xxix, including descriptions of each of the studies).

3. Jules Etienne Joseph Quicherat, *Histoire du costume en France* [*depuis les temps les plus reculés jusqu'à la fin du XVIIIe siècle*], Paris, Hachette, 1875, III–680p. Camille Enlart, *Manuel d'archéologie française*, Paris, Picard, 1916. Germain Demay, *Le Costume au moyen age, d'après les sceaux*, Paris, Dumoulin et cie, 1880 [with chapters on the outfits of kings and queens, of women, of knights and horses, of sailors, huntsmen and the clergy, as displayed on elaborate seals dating back to the Middle Ages].

4. The best drawings, because overtly schematic, are those by Nevil Truman, *Historic Costuming*, London, Pitman, 1936.

5. The history of language is not very helpful here; not only can a garment change its name without changing function, but, conversely, it can change function without a change of name. In any case, the lexicology of clothes is still very fragmentary (see Greimas, *La Mode en 1830...*, typed thesis, 1948 [republished in Greimas 2000] and Eva Rodhe Lundquist, *La Mode et son vocabulaire* [*Quelques termes de la mode féminine au moyen âge suivis dans leur évolution sémantique*, thesis], Göteborg, Wettergren & Kerber 1950,

190 p. [Editors' note: seeing language as linked to social and political change, Lundquist describes the semantic changes in fashion as 'capricious' (171)].

6. There would be a case for listing all the changes in how a garment is worn. We might find a law that says that a garment is always pushed from the inside to the outside; only psychoanalysts have treated this question so far.

7. André Varagnac, *Définition du folklore*, Paris, Société d'éditions géographiques, maritimes et coloniales, 1938, p. 21. [Editors' note: Varagnac says that national folklore is 'rare', rather than Barthes's 'never'.]

8. The birth of vestimentary deception, at the end of the fifteenth century, can be understood only if it is linked organically to an ideological transformation in the function of social 'appearances'. Quicherat himself (*Histoire du costume*, p. 330) did not hesitate in linking this with the birth of capitalism; but this type of observation is very rare.

9. Lucien Febvre, 'Le problème des divisions en histoire', in *Bulletin du Centre International de Synthèse Historique*, no. 2 December 1926, p.10 ff. [Editors' note: this is in fact not the title at all of Febvre's ideas, but part of a conference discussion based on a presentation by O. de Halecki on 'Divisions' in the history of the Middle Ages; Febvre's commentary on de Halecki's ideas is in section II (pp. 22–26), and the key passage is on pp. 24–26, where Febvre suggests that the only way to overcome the difficulty of dating periods is to 'place onself inside man – this crossroads where all influences congregrate'. This is an early example of what the *Annales* historians would go on to call a 'conjuncture'; and it is capitalism in Pirenne's *Périodes de l'histoire sociale du Capitalisme* that is Febvre's example of 'the stunning regularity of periodicity' (23); for Febvre (and the *Annales* school) the period needs to be defined as the meeting of the end of the past and the start of the future as found in human beings; but, stresses Febvre, it is churlish to suggest here a precise *end point* of course; instead, he argues, we should look for 'one of the states of momentary equilibrium, of temporary stability that are eye-catching, where it appears that, for a short instant, all things are in harmony and mutually help one another, and to look for, *in the run-up*, that which comes before

this equilibrium and which prepared it, and then following it that which slowly undoes and ruins it; there is nothing arbitrary about this kind of research' (25). And so, for Febvre, 'it is not the outside, but the inside that history should define as its "regions" [...], its historical periods' (26).]

10. On the deep regularity in fashion rhythms, see Jane Richardson and Alfred Louis Kroeber, *Three Centuries of Women's Dress Fashions. A Quantative Analysis*, Berkeley, University of California Press, 1940.

11. The return of certain forms over centuries has led to authors placing dress within the perspectives of a species of universal anthropology. On this, see Rudolf Kristian Albert Broby-Johansen, *Krop og kloer*, Copenhagen, Kultur Forlag 1953 [trans. as *Body and Clothes* by Karen Rush and Erik Friis, London, Faber, 1968], and Bernard Rudofsky, *Are Clothes Modern?*, Chicago, Paul Theobald, 1947.

12. [Editors' note: see Braudel's 1950 inaugural lecture at the Collège de France, published as 'Position de l'histoire en 1950 (1)' in F. Braudel, *Ecrits sur l'histoire*, Paris, Flammarion 1969, pp.15–38 (p. 24); trans. as 'The Situation of History in 1950' in Fernand Braudel, *On History*, trans. Sarah Matthews, Chicago University Press, 1980: 'Though we must of course be clear that social time does not flow at one even rate, but goes at a thousand different paces, swift or slow, which bear almost no relation to the day-to-day rhythm of a chronicle or of traditional history' (12). See also 'Histoire et sciences sociales: la longue durée', in *Annales* 4, Oct–Dec 1958 (*On History*, 25–54).]

13. For this discussion, see, above all, J.-C. Flügel, *The Psychology of Clothes*, London, Hogarth Press, 1950 [1930], ch. 1, and Hilaire and Meyer Hiler, *Bibliography of Costume*, New York, H. W. Wilson Co., 1939, preface. On the desire for modesty, apart from those cited, Pearl Binder, *Muffs and Morals*, London, G. G. Harrap, 1953, and Erik Peterson, *Pour une théologie du vêtement* [French trans. M.-J. Congar], Lyon, Ed. De l'Abeille, 1943.

14. Georges Gurvitch, *La Vocation actuelle de la sociologie [Vers une sociologie différentielle]*, Paris, PUF, 1950, ch. 1 [editors' note: 'Les Faux Problèmes de la sociologie au XIXe siècle', 19–48, in which Gurvitch considers the following problems as irrelevant to twentieth-century sociology: the fate of humanity; order and

progress; conflict between individual and society; the opposition between the psychic and the social; what is the predominant factor; establishing sociological laws; Gurvitch prefers sociology to study depth, a micro-sociology using studies of groupings, and he valorizes the collective conscience and moral theory in Durkheim and Bergson's sociology, as well as a highly relativist and 'hyper-empiricist' version of Marxian theory].

15. [Editors' note: in relation to the Roman *penula* or *lacerna*, Quicherat says that 'one wore this only to protect oneself from the rain, and on travels and in the countryside, rather than in the city (in the city, one wore a toga)' (29).]

16. It is clear that the more standardized the manufacturing, the stronger the vestimentary system. On this see the observations by Georges Friedmann on factories producing the waistcoat and the jacket, in *Le Travail en miettes*, Paris, Gallimard, 1956 [trans. as *The Anatomy of Work. The Implications of Specialisation*, by Wyatt Rawson, London, Heinemann, 1961].

17. Ferdinand de Saussure, *Cours de linguistique générale*, Paris, Payot, 1949, 4th ed. [trans. as *Course in General Linguistics*, by Wade Baskin, eds Charles Bally, Albert Sechehaye, Albert Riedlinger, London, Peter Owen, 1959]. Here we prefer the formulation of structuralism by Saussure to the narrower one by his epigones in the Prague School; Saussure's is more historical, much closer to Durkheimism. As for the possibility of extrapolating Saussurism to disciplines other than linguistics, this is implied in Saussurism itself, based as it is on a postulate that has a general epistemological significance.

18. Stephen Ullmann, *Précis de semantique française*, Paris, PUF, 1952 [first published as *The Principles of Semantics*, Glasgow, Jackson, 1951].

19. Nikolai Sergeevich Trubetskoy, *Principes de phonologie*, trans. by J. Cantineau, Paris, Klincksieck, 1949 [trans. as *Principles of Phonology*, by Christiane A. M. Baltaxe, Berkeley, University of California Press, 1969].

20. As a working hypothesis, we propose to classify *dressing objects* in the following way: (1) individual dimensions of the garment, in relation to the size of the wearer; (2) degree and particularities of how worn-out, scruffy or dirty; (3) pieces or items missing;

(4) non-usage (buttons not done up, rolled-up sleeves, etc.); (5) pure protection, not formalized (improvised outfit); choice of colours (except for ritualized colours: mourning, marriage, uniforms, tartans, etc.); (7) circumstantial derivations for an item's deployment; (8) non-stereotyped acts of usage particular to the wearer; (9) anomalies, or allowances, in the dress object.

21. We can now suggest the following refinements:

I. *Garments*: (1) forms, substances, formalized or ritualized colours; (2) fixed circumstantial usage; (3) stereotyped acts of dressing; (4) particular ways of wearing a garment; (5) distribution of accessories (pockets, buttons, etc.).

II. *Systems or arrangements*: (1) apparent global system ('uniform'); (2) a partial system forming a unit of usage or of meaning; (3) incompatibility of items; (4) matching of items; (5) the play on whether an item is worn externally or internally; (6) dressing that is reconstituted artificially to create meanings or for the use of a group (outfits for the theatre or cinema).

22. On this, see A. J. Greimas, 'L'actualité du saussurisme', in *Le Français Moderne*, July 1956, p. 202 [republished in Greimas 2000, 371–82].

23. The 'model' or 'cover girl' represents the tightest unity of a dressing object with a dress object: in any collection of clothes there are traces of dressing (dimensions of the wearer); however, these traces are tiny because the real aim of the dressing here is to display an outfit.

24. Sir George H. Darwin, 'Development in Dress', *Macmillan's Magazine*, September, 1872 [pp. 410–416; recently republished in Stern 2004, 96-104]. [Editors' note: analysing men's clothing only, George H. Darwin sees a 'strong analogy' between development of dress and that of organisms, and he uses evolutionary theory – natural selection 'and associated doctrines of development' – to show that dress also has 'almost infinite ramifications' in other areas of study (416); he considers utility as a determining factor in clothing forms, and fashion (or 'the love of novelty') as having 'no distant analogy to "sexual selection" ' in the 'Descent of Man', in which both animals and dress forms maintain 'remnants of former stages of development', preserving 'a tattered record of the history of their evolution' (410); he then traces these analogies through

styles in hat, coat and boot; nothing, concludes Darwin junior, is devoid of a cause, 'the observation of even common things of everyday life may be made less trivial than at first sight it might appear' (416).]

25. This is what André Georges Haudricourt and Alphonse Juillard have tried to do in phonology (*Essai pour une histoire structurale du phonétisme français*, Paris, Klincksieck, 1949).

26. *Les Fonctions psychologiques et les oeuvres*, Paris J. Vrin, 1948, ch. II. [Editors' note: the chapter 'Le Signe', pp. 75–115, is an early and useful explanation and application of Saussurian linguistics to literature.]

27. The bibliography of these enquiries and questionnaires on the psychology of motivations in clothes (already old, admittedly) can be found in Estelle De Young Barr, *A Psychological Analysis of Fashion Motivation*, New York, 1954 [1934].

28. Flügel distinguishes nine types of garments according to the psychology of the wearer: (1) rebellious type; (2) resigned type; (3) unemotional type; (4) prudish type; (5) duty type; (6) protected type; (7) supported type; (8) sublimated type; (9) self-satisfied type (*The Psychology of Clothes*, p. 96).

29. These two aspects of psychoanalytical explanation can be understood by the ways we understand starching (Flügel, ibid.): it is explained by psychoanalysis either as an extension of the personality or as a phallic symbol. However, outside of the psychoanalytical perspective, Western dress never really has any symbols (one of the rare examples would be medieval bi-partism, a symbol of psychic division); so dress is based entirely on an order of *signs* and not of *symbols*, that is to say there is no motivational link in dress between the signified and the signifier.

30. It goes without saying that the play in vestimentary signs is heavily dependent on the standing of the wearer as an index of their standard of living.

# 2

# *Language and Clothing*[1]

At first sight, human clothing is a very promising subject to research or reflect upon: it is a complete phenomenon, the study of which requires at any one time a history, an economy, an ethnology, a technology and maybe even, as we will see in a moment, a type of linguistics. But above all, as an object of *appearance*,[2] it flatters our modern curiosity about social psychology, inviting us to go beyond the obsolete limits of the individual and of society: what is interesting in clothing is that it seems to participate to the greatest depth in the widest sociality. We can imagine that researchers using the most recent social methods – psychoanalysis, Marxism or structuralism – must naturally be interested in it, especially given that clothing is at first glance an everyday object, and is thus one of those most prominent of observed features in society that stimulates our keenest contemporary research.

Given this ideal set of interests, the published research results are themselves actually rather meagre. If we look only at the bibliographical indications, which are as abundant as they are anarchic[3], clothing is a disappointing subject; even to the extent to which it seems to invite a unifying epistemology, it is elusive. Here it is a picturesque spectacle (in countless albums for the general public), there a psychological phenomenon – but it is still never truly an object of sociological inquiry; the best reflections it has generated remain incidental: they are those by writers and philosophers, perhaps because they alone are sufficiently free from its perceived triviality.[4] But if we move away from the realm of the aphorism, towards that of sociological description, we find in the very definition of clothing a methodological difficulty, which I would like to try to pin down by way of a quick history of the work so far.

This history is relatively recent. Of course, since the Renaissance there have been works on clothing: these either had archaeological aims (with ancient clothing for example), or else they were inventories of clothes governed by social conditions: these inventories are veritable lexicons, linking vestimentary systems very tightly either to anthropological states (sex, age, marital status) or to social ones (bourgeoisie, nobility, peasantry, etc.), but it is clear that this sort of lexicon of clothing was possible only in a society which was starkly hierarchical, in which fashion was part of a real social ritual.[5] On this subject I would like to cite an important work – Larmessin's seventeenth-century *Costumes grotesques* – because it represents an imaginary state not unlike the superlative case that is this vestimentary lexicon. For each profession Larmessin composed a form of dress whose elements were borrowed as if in a dream from the tools of the relevant activity, which were then arranged into a sort of general line or signifying *gestalt* (the process is not dissimilar to the paintings of Arcimboldo): it is a kind of frenetic pan-symbolism, a creation which is both poetic and intelligible, in which the profession is represented by its imaginary essence: calm forms for the pastry-maker, serpentine for the apothecary, pointed for the fireworks manufacturer, rounded and humped for the potter, etc.: in this fantasy, clothing ends up absorbing Man completely, the worker is anatomically assimilated to the respective instruments and in the end it is an alienation which here is described poetically: Larmessin's workers are robots *avant la lettre*.

Dress history did not really begin until Romanticism and then it was undertaken by theatre specialists; it is because actors wanted to play their roles in the clothes of the period that painters and designers began to strive systematically towards historical accuracy in appearances (clothing, sets, furniture and props), in short that denoted precisely by the term 'costume'.[6] So what was beginning to be reconstituted here was essentially *roles*, and the reality being sought was a purely theatrical one: myths such as kings, queens and lords were being openly reconstituted; the first consequence of this was that clothing was only ever analysed anthologically, as if it were a compilation; it was the attribute of a particular race, selected for romantic theatre: it was as if ordinary people had never been dressed; the second consequence, and perhaps more significant methodologically, was that the costume designer's attention was drawn towards the picturesque, and not towards the design principle, towards the stage prop and not towards the system. Perhaps, paradoxically, the opportunities offered by drawing have profoundly harmed dress history: graphic, spontaneous representation removed all speculative work; an imperfectly established generality was being actualized on the spot. This is why the most methodologically sound illustrations are, in my view, those drawings which are overtly schematic, those which aim to arrive at a state of principle, or abstraction, with regard to the vestimentary system of a particular epoch, such as those by Nevil Truman in *Historic Costuming*.

Apart from the theatre painters, however, there was a rather interesting whole literature on clothing in the first half of the nineteenth century, known as the *Physiologies*.[7] The flourishing of these short monographs is well known, with their generally playful tone, covering the most varied aspects of what we would call today daily life, from the office employee to the tobacconist. There are a number of *physiologies* of clothing (the Corset, the Tie, the Shirt, the Glove, the Hat).[8] What is most interesting in these dissertations is their sociological aspect: the great movement within masculine dress towards standardization and democratization launched by the Revolution and inspired in form by reference to the austerity of Quaker dress, was bringing about a whole revision of vestimentary values; seemingly *déclassé*, clothing could signal social distinctions only via a new value, namely that of *distinction*; inspired by dandyism, this was the role of the *physiologies*: to teach the aristocrat how to distinguish himself from the proletarian or from the bourgeois by the *manner* in which an item, now formally undifferentiated, was worn; as one of the *Physiologies* puts it, the tie has replaced the sword: in all of these opuscules found in the *Physiologies* an outline of an axiology of clothing is beginning to take shape. In the second half of the nineteenth century the Romantic spirit gave way to archaeological research: clothing was now to be described by (mainly medievalist) scholars,[9] item by item and according to a chronology borrowed from the traditional narrative of History (or 'King's History'). To the extent that this work is important, it is the methodological gaps which come into focus: these historians scrupulously established a history of items but not one of systems; thanks to them we know to within a year when a particular garment appeared – but much less when it disappeared, as inaugural phenomena are always much more marked than those in the process of obsolescence; we even know in the majority of cases what was the contingent cause of a particular fashion; but we have only a very scant knowledge of how the structures change; for a vestimentary structure is not a sum of items in which a few have changed according to circumstances; here, as elsewhere, a structure is defined both by what is legal (what is allowed and what is not) and by the sorts of play within this legality. Historicism has not contributed to a true description of clothing systems; it considers an item merely as an event, where the problem is then simply one of being able to put a date on it. The result is that historical clothing appears to be a collection of available items, and not an approved set of combinations; in short it is facts and not values that have been collated; this problem is made all the more complicated by the well-known uncertainties about periodization in history:[10] either we describe reigns, as if the king were the exclusive wearer of clothing, its ritual founder, but this would introduce anarchy into the vestimentary system itself because the temporal unity of a system is not necessarily the same as that of political history; or else we describe the permanent features and changes of global forms, but this can be achieved only by using a structuralist approach of which historicism is unaware. This is the unresolved problem: to be honest, we cannot blame historians for this if you consider that a neighbouring science such as linguistics, though extensively researched by generations of specialists, has only just barely begun to confront the difficult problem of the links between diachrony and synchrony.[11]

However, since the end of the nineteenth century, there have been a certain number of illustrated works, in the form of historical popularizations, which have tended to place clothing in relation to a reality external to its form, in short to postulate a transcendence of dress. These comparisons have assumed a sort of equivalence between one form and other forms (for example, between two 'styles', between one in clothing and one in architecture, or in furniture) – the most convincing of these works on this subject is by Hansen, which is cited at the start of this article – or between a form and the *spirit* of a particular time, the *moral character* of a period or the Zeitgeist of a civilization. None of these attempts ever really gets beyond the boundaries of tautology: a 'style' is arbitrarily inferred from an item of clothing, this style is then linked to other styles which are just as arbitrary and then, to finish, we are all impressed by the close relationship of the forms. We know, however, that a form does not signify anything *in itself* (unless we go back to a universal symbolism of a Freudian variety), for the good reason that forms are finite in number and meanings infinite: in any primary formal order, only the functions, and not the substances, can carry meaning. Consequently in any vestimentary system one is as unlikely to find a purely historical, semelfactive phenomenon as to find a purely anthropological, eternal one; both postulations have existed in the history of clothing: as much as certain writers have excelled at locating styles historically, others have gone to great efforts, with no less success, to bring vestimentary variations down to a few simple forms, tirelessly repeated by human history; for some people, the *hennin* [steeple headdress] expresses the gothic tower in a way which is in some sense irreversible, for others, what is significant about the history of clothing is that one can already see very modern bikinis on the frescoes at Pompeii.[12]

Through these hypotheses the idea of a true semiology of clothing is gradually emerging. We need to link clothing to something. But to what? And how? The historical trend has been followed, by and large, by the psychological trend. The term of reference here is no longer the spirit or style of a period, but the *psyche* of the person wearing the clothing: clothing is supposed to express a psychological depth. Here there are two routes to take. The first is an already dated collection of work, and very modest in its pretensions because it mainly concerns questionnaires given to students at a few American universities. This work is all based on the psychology of motivation: the idea is to define and classify personal motives which encourage the purchase of an item of clothing. This research is barely distinguishable from the marketing polls carried out periodically by professional cloth-ing companies: the role of advertising, the proximity of the shops, 'fashion tips' from friends, the effect of shop windows, etc., the hierarchy of qualities required of the item bought (durability, taste, degree of fashionability, comfort, etc.). It is quite clear that this is barely a psychology but at best a rudimentary psycho-sociology which can know nothing of the potential of phenomenological or psychoanalytical descriptions; the central notion in this psychology is *self-expression*, as if the fundamental function of clothing were to bring together and solidify the self confronted by a society wishing to swallow it up: it is possible that there is something specifically American about this interpretation.[13]

The second route in these psychologies of clothing is psycho-analytical. For this I would first suggest Kiener's recent book, even though it is more gestaltist than psychoanalytical in inspiration. Kiener attempts to link clothing to a kind of *esprit* of the human body, as if anatomical form were the basis of clothing across a series of links and of distances and the meaning of which varies with history. But, with the exception of proper psychopathological studies on transvestism, the classic work, in terms of a psychoanalysis of clothing, is by Flügel; indeed its classic status is based more on its breadth of information than on the sharpness of its analyses; it is a fairly eclectic work which uses traditional analytical concepts within a 'psychological' framework (the motives of modesty, pro-tection and ornamentation); the symbolism proposed remains cursory and narrowly analogous (for example, starching is seen as a phallic symbol). Despite these limitations there is probably in Flügel the origins of two interesting hypotheses: firstly, that clothing is a compromise between the fear of, and the desire for, nudity, which would make clothing part of the very process of neurosis, that is both display and mask; perhaps intuitively here, we can see the dialectical nature of clothing, in which there seems to be an infinite and cir-cular exchange from the wearer to the group and from the group to the wearer; a second interesting hypothesis in Flügel suggests that analytical censorship actually corresponds to the sociological notion of social control: in other words, clothing would seem to be less an index (or a symptom) but more a form of communication. So here we are, after this brief panorama of histories of clothing, encouraged to posit clothing in terms of meaning; thus a whole literature, with diverse inspirations and qualities, but across which clothing is already felt as a *value-for*, has led us to this point. However it was a structuralist, Trubetskoy, who was the first to posit openly the linguistic nature of clothing.

In an incidental remark in his *Principles of* Phonology,[14] Trubetskoy suggests applying the Saussurian distinction between *langue* and *parole* to clothing; like *langue*, clothing would be an institutional system, abstract and defined by its functions, and from which the individual wearer would draw their apparel, each time actualizing a normative virtuality. Trubetskoy adduced as a phenomenon of dressing (that is, *parole*) the individual dimensions of an item of clothing, its degree of wear and dirtiness, and as a phenomenon of dress (that is, *langue*) the difference, no matter how tiny, between the clothing of unmarried girls and that of married women in any society. I would suggest developing this opposition in the following way: dressing (*parole*) would include the individual dimensions of the clothing item, the degree of wear, of disorder or dirtiness, partial absences of items (buttons not done up, sleeves not rolled down, etc.), improvised clothes (ad hoc protection), the choice of colours (except those colours ritualized in mourning, marriage, tartans, uniforms), the incidental derivations of how an item is used, the wearer's particular way of wearing clothes. Dress (*langue*), which is always abstract and only requiring a description that is either verbal or schematic,[15] would include the ritualized forms, substances and colours, fixed uses, stereotyped modes, the tightly controlled distribution of accessories (buttons, pockets, etc.), obvious systems ('ceremonial' dress), the incongruences and incompatibilities of items, the controlled game of undergarments and overgarments, and finally those dress phenomena which are artificially reconstituted in order to signify (theatre and film costumes). I think that this application of the Saussurian distinction to clothing is very valuable; this application allows research into clothing to monitor constantly the institutional and sociological character of its object; and, using facts which seem at first to be ambiguous and drawing only confusedly on clothes and dressing and on the individual and society, it throws a clear light: it is because Richardson and Kroeber defined the exact sense of the limits in which the proportions of a item of clothing stopped being a part of dressing and became part of dress, that they were able to establish, in a work well known to structuralists, the regularity in the rhythms of fashion evident for the last three centuries in women's clothing.[16] Finally, the Saussurian distinction allows us to describe with accuracy all the truly dialectical movements which govern the incessant exchanges between institutional clothing and clothing that is actually put on: how an outfit becomes clothes (in the general case of women's fashion, diffused into clothing habits by real models); how clothes in their turn become part of outfits (in the case of individual usage becoming picked up collectively by imitation, fads and crazes, which are so frequent in dandyism).

Now that the distinction between clothing and dress has been ascertained, we must ask what actually signifies in dress. Dress is *a priori* a kind of *text without end* in which it is necessary to learn how to delimit the signifying units, and this is very difficult. Technology is of very little help here: a unit of manufacture or of purchase, in short what is called the article (a shirt, a skirt, a jacket), is not necessarily a signifying unit. Clearly meaning is not located in the finished object, it can be found in a tiny detail or in a complex outfit. Except in cases of flagrant eccentricity, the item signifies nothing. Furthermore, it has been a long time since our clothing represented any analogical link between signifier and signified except when we have recourse to a universal symbolism of the unconscious sort; one of the last analogies in our Western dress was in the Middle Ages when there was the particoloured outfit worn by madmen, a symbol of psychic division; since then, forms seem to have followed an evolution which is properly internal, removed from all symbolic reference (and this constitutes another of the lessons of the work of Richardson and Kroeber). On the one hand we have the signifieds (for example: youthfulness, intellectualism, respectability, bohemianism, etc.) and on the other signifiers which are abstract, highly mobile, arbitrary forms, (and which we could even say are 'an-iconic'), but without the link between the signifiers and the signifieds, that is the meaning, ever losing its normative, threatening, terroristic character.

This probably means that the semiology of clothing is not lexical but syntactic. It is because meaning is neither motivated, nor coded, by an ancestral grammar in the way that clothing was in ancient oriental societies, that we are forced to look for clothing's unit of meaning not in whole, isolated items, but in true functions, oppositions, distinctions and congruences. These are probably quite closely analogous to the units of phonology. So, as in phonology, we should submit the vestimentary continuum to a series of *commutation tests*, in order to isolate the units that really do hold meaning (the *semes*); to take a rather crude example, does putting leather buttons on a jacket give it a new meaning? It is likely that simple oppositions (leather buttons/other buttons) are only remotely meaningful; it is the 'combinatory variants', true functions of functions, which are able to achieve the status of being meaningful (for example: tweed/leather buttons/lighter-pocket, etc.). Of course, the absence of elements can play a role which is meaningful (for example, not wearing a tie): the vestimentary sign can be expressed as the degree zero, it is never null. Conversely, we should learn to decipher the accumulation of signifiers: in the majority of outfits there is a *redundancy* of messages, the study of which could lead to a structural definition of taste.

The inventory of the signifying elements of clothing posited here in a purely hypothetical way has never been undertaken by anybody. Maybe the task is premature (we would need a vast information apparatus, if only in order to list all the vestimentary 'texts': observations, analyses, continual updatings, which could only be done by a team of researchers). Maybe we should start with the crudest of analyses about which I would like to make a few observations. The major difficulty in the analytical deciphering of 'everyday' clothing is its syntactic nature: the signified is only ever expressed in this regard via signifiers 'in operation', meaning is an indissoluble whole that tends to evaporate as soon as one divides it up. Now luckily, there is an artificial form of clothing in which the signifieds are separated *a priori* from the signifiers, and this is fashion clothing that is presented in both graphic and descriptive form in newspapers and magazines.[17] Here, the signified is given explicitly, even before the signifier is *named* (an autumn skirt, a woman's suit for five o'clock in the afternoon, etc.); it is as if you were being given a very complex text to read, one made up of subtle norms but to which one had the good fortune at the same time to have the key: luckily, fashion that is written or drawn brings the semiologist back towards a lexical state of the vestimentary signs. We are probably talking about an elaborated language, a logo-technics, whose signifieds are largely unreal, the stuff of dreams. However, this does not matter, since what is being sought here is, first, a field which is sufficiently crude, sufficiently *loaded*, so that meaning is seen to be functioning in slow motion as it were, in its decomposed stages. A semiology of printed fashion must ensure that it is able to deal legitimately with the greatest danger threatening any semiology of the first degree: the unjustified objectification of the signifieds. On the contrary, with written fashion being a semiological system of the second degree it becomes not only legitimate, but even necessary, to separate the signified from the signifier and to give to the signified the very weight of an object. In other words, and to pick up on a definition that I outlined in a previous essay,[18] printed fashion functions, semiologically speaking, like a true mythology of clothing: it is even because the vestimentary signified is here objectified, thickened, that fashion is mythic. So it is this mythology of clothing (one could also say its utopia) that needs to be the first stage of a vestimentary linguistics.

## Notes

1. Published in *Critique* 142 (March) 1959, 243–52; *Oeuvres complètes* vol. 1, 793–800. A review of: J. Flügel, *The Psychology of Clothes*, London, Hogarth Press, 1950; Franz Kiener, *Kleidung, Mode und Mensch* [*Versuch einer psychologischen Deutung*], Munich, Ernst Reinhardt Verlag 1956; Henny Harald Hansen, *Histoire du costume*, trans. from Danish by Jacqueline Puissant, Flammarion, 1956 [first English edition as *Costume Cavalcade: 685 Examples of Costume in Colour*, London, Methuen, 1956; a richly illustrated but rather simplistic view of clothes history]; Nevil Truman, *Historic Costume*, London, Isaac Pitman & Son, 1936.

2. [Editors' note: *paraître* – 'appearance' – is a word strongly linked to the renaissance philosopher Michel de Montaigne.]

3. See René Colas, *Bibliographie générale du costume et de la mode*, Paris, Librairie Colas, 1932–1933, 2 vol. in-4⁰; Hilaire and Meyer Hiler, *Bibliography of Costume*, New York, H.W. Wilson Co., 1939.

4. Amongst others: Carlyle, Michelet, Balzac.

5. The best ethnological observations on this subject are probably those by Marcel Granet on ancient China.

6. *Costume*: 'Truth of usages, clothes etc., reproduced in works of art', 1676, Félibien. [Editors' note: see André Félibien, *Conférences de l'Académie Royale de peinture et de sculpture* (Paris, Frédéric Léonard, 1676).]

7. The list of these *Physiologies* can be found at the Bibliothèque Nationale, in the general catalogue for the History of France, under 'Li'.

8. [Editors' note: see Balzac's 'La cravate c'est l'homme'; Balzac was the anonymous author of *L'Art de mettre sa cravate*, and, says Pearl Binder (*Muffs and Morals*, London, G.G. Harrap, 1953, p. 48), was fascinated by the many ways of tying the cravat – *à la Byron, en cascade, à la paresseuse*, and the tight, stuffed and stiffened *cravate de bureaucrate* satirized by Daumier. And, in the first half of the nineteenth century, it mirrored the shifting social stresses in the France of that period.]

9. Notably Jules Etiennce Joseph Quicherat, *Histoire du costume en France*, Paris, Hachette, 1875. Camille Enlart, *Manuel d'archéologie française*, Paris, Picard, 1916 (t. III). Germain Demay, *Le Costume au moyen age, d'après les sceaux*, Paris, Dumoulin et cie, 1880.

10. Lucien Febvre, 'Le problème des divisions en histoire', in the *Bulletin du Centre International de Synthèse Historique*, no. 2, December 1926. [Editors' note: but see note 9 in Chapter 1 here, 'History and Sociology of Clothing'.]

11. André Georges Haudricourt and Alphonse Julliard, *Essai pour une histoire structurale du phonétisme français*, Klincksieck, 1949.

12. On this see Rudolph Kristian Albert Broby-Johansen, *Krop og kloer*, Copenhagen, 1953 and Bernard Rudofsky, *Are Clothes Modern?* [*An Essay on Contemporary Apparel*], Chicago, Paul Theobald 1947; these two works contain numerous illustrations that tend to show the permanence of vestimentary forms.

13. A bibliography of these American works can be found in Estelle De Young Barr, *A Psychological Analysis of Fashion Motivation*, New York, 1954 [1934].

14. Nikolai Sergeevich Trubetskoy, *Principes de phonologie*, trans. by J. Cantineau, Paris, Klincksieck, 1949, p.19; trans. as *Principles of Phonology*, by Christine A.M. Baltaxe, Berkeley, University of California Press, 1969.

15. Fashion photography poses an interesting methodological problem; in Saussurian terms, it represents a kind of ideal confusion between dressing and dress, as do the clothes in presentations of collections.

16. Jane Richardson and Alfred Louis Kroeber, *Three Centuries of Women's [Dress] Fashions, A Quantative Analysis*, Berkeley, University of California Press, 1940.

17. Another artificial from of clothing which presents a most valuable disjuncture between the signifieds and the signifiers is liturgical dress.

18. *Mythologies*, Paris, Seuil, 1957 [1970], the final part: 'Myth, Today'.

# 3

# *Towards a Sociology of Dress*[1]

I suggested in this journal[2] that, if we exclude the numerous histories of clothes, the majority of which merely repeat each other, then works on clothing overall are rare; and since this is a vast subject, barely explored, and in which there is a permanent temptation towards futility, any serious attempt or claim to synthesize clothing is eagerly seized upon. There is no lack of such intentions in Fr. Kiener's work.[3] But I doubt whether this study provides anything really new for those who have read the work by Flügel which, despite (or, perhaps, because of) its bias, is unrivalled to this day.[4]

To understand Kiener's tentativeness we have to remind ourselves of Flügel's bias. Flügel located himself clearly within a psychoanalytical perspective; he has used the lexicon of Freudian symbols to describe human clothing as the ambiguous expression, both mask and advertisement, of the unconscious self. Even if we reject Freudian symbolism, his work remains doubly valuable: first, because he has brought together the essential elements of clothing phenomena, pulling them out of history, folklore, literature or contemporary society, in short putting order into what everyone more or less knows (for here there is a subtle difficulty for all work on clothing: how to give objective value to something which seems insignificant because it is experienced subjectively); second, because he has explicitly conceived clothing as a *value-for*, that is as a form of meaning (where the signified is the deep *psyche*); for the first time, clothing was now liberated from the triangle of motivations (protection, modesty, ornamentation) in which it had been locked, and reached the status of message, an element in a semiological system: in this sense, and in spite of his strict obedience to analysis, Flügel makes clothing much more into communication than expression.

Like Flügel, Kiener begins by discussing the old motivations (protection, modesty, ornamentation), from which, rather eclectically, he retains certain elements. But his main point is to posit clothing as the expression of the body,[5] from which he gleans the body's successive modes of being; and this inclines him to organize the main parts of his book following a purely anatomical schema:[6] head, trunk, pelvis, legs, etc., and then to consider, for each of these parts, all the diverse 'motives' for which men have covered themselves; his attempt is a bit like the great description of the French language by Damourette and Pichon: it has the same encyclopaedic aims, the same qualities (an abundance of data, finely detailed analyses), and the same faults (disorder beneath a semblance of order, continual confusion between synchrony and diachrony).

It is this 'naturalist' postulate that leaves Kiener lagging behind in relation to Flügel. Certainly his material is substantial, gleaned from a wide variety of sources (myths, history, folklore, sayings, legends, jokes, dreams, anecdotes), all presented in a rather pell-mell fashion but in such a way that the analysis is constantly threatened with confusion and with banality, since everything is considered as a 'detail' whilst nothing is regarded as exemplary. But above all it is the principle of interpretation that is disappointing. Kiener is aiming towards a 'psychology' (but does not state which one). Unfortunately, as Kiener gradually links the body and clothing, the psychology evaporates, as if in a conjuring trick. One may wish to contest the Freudian psychology that Flügel uses, but it does have the merit of being sufficiently structured so as to set up a fruitful working hypothesis. But by constantly drawing clothing back into a kind of 'natural meaning' emanating from the body, Kiener is, despite himself, forced into stating truisms; the majority of his analyses are veritable tautologies in which the body is the body rather like the way in which ancient graphology used to suggest that limp handwriting was indicative of a limp personality. To say for example that a short item of clothing is chosen because it is practical is of very little interest unless you then submit the notion of *practical* to a historical and ideological analysis that reveals the relative nature of such a term: for what is of interest is not the diversity of clothing items but the relativity of the values that they signify. There is in all this a sort of latent essentialism that cuts explanation short, with

Kiener having recourse to a set of essences that remind you of the 'soporific' effects of opium (the essence of Woman, the 'spirit of the times', the 'life instinct', the 'need for change', the 'slowing down in growth', etc.).

Certainly, nothing is simplistic in Kiener's book; he has recognized, if not exploited, the possibilities of a phenomenological analysis of clothing, of what he calls the *Kleider-Ich*, the 'Me Clothing' (even though his observations on the extension of the self and on vestimentary eroticism are already to be found largely in Flügel).[7] Furthermore, his encyclopaedic sense and his thirst for tiny facts and contradictory details (and the history of clothing is indeed a series of 'inversions') give his work a kind of relativist dimension. But the price he pays is a contradiction which he resolves badly: on the one hand, he resorts constantly, but anarchically, to history (without, moreover, taking social distinctions sufficiently into account), to the extent that clothing, in its diachrony, becomes a monotonous series of ruptures, a disordered succession of opposites; and on the other, his plan, the very aim of his work, postulates a 'natural' anthropology, a kind of psychological essence of the human body, which, if it were true, would logically lead to a universal form of clothing, or at least to a very weak variation and not an absolute variation as is the case in our world: if the neck is a part of the body that must be protected, how is it that *every* form possible, from covering to revealing the neck, has existed? There is a contradiction here between history and 'Nature', a hiatus between a strict finality of the organ and the diversity of clothing experiments, and the law of heterogony alone (which Kiener borrows from Wundt) is not adequate to explain it.

All in all, what is valuable in this book is the detail: in order to have a historical and anthropological inventory of clothing phenomena there must be a lot of culture, supplied by very varied sources. Many of Kiener's analyses of items are not only brilliant but also exciting, encouraging us to think of problems which go far beyond the detail. Unfortunately, what we really need in this subject are systematic attempts to consider clothing as a structure and not as an anarchic collection of tiny events. Furthermore I doubt whether the very notion of an item could withstand such structuration. For what interests us in items of clothing is essentially the links between them; what we need is a description that is more functional than substantial. Now the example of linguistics (and especially phonology) suggests that we cannot describe a reality as a structure unless we modify the very idea of those phenomena that compete with each other to form a function: phonological 'phenomena' are very different from phonetic 'phenomena'. The day when the study of clothing moves from, shall I say, the lexical to the syntactical, is the day when the majority of the 'phenomena' collected by the psychology of clothing will be useless because they will suddenly have no meaning.

## Notes

1. Published in *Annales*, March–April 1960, 404–7; *Oeuvres complètes* vol. 1, 853–55. A review of Fr. Kiener, *Le Vêtement, la mode et l'homme. Essai d'interprétation psychologique.*

2. *Annales* 3, July–September 1957, 741–52. [See chapter 1 here, 'History and Sociology of Clothing. Some Methodological Observations'].

3. F. Kiener, *Le Vêtement, la mode et l'homme. Essai d'interprétation psychologique*, Munich: Reinhardt, 1956.

4. J.-C. Flügel, *The Psychology of Clothes*, London, Hogarth Press, 3rd edition, 1950.

5. Kiener considers his research to be part of the 'science of expression' (*Ausdruckskunde*).

6. Aiming to describe clothing from a technological point of view, André Leroi-Gourhan was right to adopt a classification system based not on the parts of the body but where the items rested (*Milieu et techniques*, Paris, Albin Michel, 1950 [1945] [see the chapter 'le vêtement', 209–53, with ample illustrations by Leroi-Gourhan].

7. When Kiener defines ornamentation as a 'role' (*I am what I make of myself*), he is proposing a very rich line of research which could benefit from certain developments in phenomenology (there are certain elements of this in Sartre's *Saint Genet*) and in psychopathology (I am thinking in particular of Roland Kuhn, *Phénoménologie du masque. A travers le test de Rorschach*, Paris, Desclée

de Brouwer, 1957 [trans. from German by Jacqueline Verdeaux, with a preface by Gaston Bachelard; it uses Rorschach's test in which patients are asked to draw and identify faces to reveal psychological disorders and traits]). Kiener makes another, much more interesting, point about the intellectual 'role' of the person who wears glasses.

# Part II

# Systems and Structures

# 4

# 'Blue is in Fashion This Year'

## A Note on Research into Signifying Units in Fashion Clothing[1]

1. When I read in a fashion magazine that *the accessory makes spring-time*, that *this* women's suit (of which I have a photograph in front of me) has a *young and slinky look*, or that *blue is in fashion this year*, I cannot but see a semantic structure in these suggestions: in every case, and whatever the metaphorical detours taken by the wording, I see imposed upon me a link of equivalence between a concept (*spring, youth, fashion this year*) and a form (*the accessory, this suit*, the colour *blue*), between a signified and a signifier.

Of course, we are not talking about a rigorous production of meaning: the link is neither obligatory nor sufficiently motivated. If it is suggested to me: *for a teatime dance at Juan-les-Pins, a lavish, straight neckline*, or *for a lunchtime party in Deauville, a soft canezou*, we have here a doubly feeble link – the teatime dance does not require such a neckline, nor the Normandy lunch a canezou. Nevertheless, there is an expressive affinity between the two terms in the link I make, the beginnings of a tautology: one term *calls for* the other, the link is like a quotation. At the very least I can see that there is *meaning* between them; it is almost as if the fashion magazine were linking a certain domain (a daytime party, the cool climate of Normandy) with another (warm and light materials, enveloping and elegant forms), using the most elementary of signifying processes. I am not yet certain that clothing does carry meaning; but I am right at least to apply a linguistic method of analysis to it: it is this conformity of the method to its object that will *prove* to me the signifying nature of fashion clothing,[2] rather than the consciousness of its wearers, which is to some extent an alienated one.

2. For fashion-magazine rhetoric is actively engaged in hiding the semantic nature of the links that it proposes. Sometimes the rhetoric presents the signifieds (fashionability, slinkiness, springtime) as qualities inherent to the forms it proposes, suggesting that there is a kind of physical causality between fashion and the colour blue, between the accessory and spring.[3] Elsewhere, the rhetoric reduces the signified to a simple utilitarian function (a coat *for* the journey). Whether causality or finality, the phrasing used in a fashion magazine always has a subtle tendency to transform the linguistic status of the clothing item into one of naturalness or usefulness, to invest an effect or a function in the sign; in both cases, it is all about changing an arbitrary link into a natural property or a technical affinity, in short providing fashion creations with the guarantee of being eternal or empirically necessary. The fashion magazine, it has to be said, never uses anything but *sign-functions*: the function can never be separated from its sign. A raincoat protects against rain, but also and indissociably, it points to its status as raincoat. This is moreover the fundamental status of clothes: an item of clothing that is purely functional is conceivable only outside of any notion of society – as soon as an item is actually manufactured, it inevitably becomes an element in semiology.

3. The first task, then, is to reduce the phraseology of the fashion magazine (which does not mean that we will not later have to re-interpret it, and at that point in a mythological way). What becomes apparent then are the simple links, belonging to a single model (which allows us to collate), between signifieds and signifiers. These links are simple, but they are not pure; for the signifiers are always part of a physical world which is the clothing content, the fragment of bodily space occupied by the clothing item (a woman's suit, a pleat, a clip brooch, gilt buttons, etc.); whereas the signifieds (romantic, nonchalant, cocktail party, countryside, skiing, feminine youth, etc.) are given to me necessarily via the written word, via a literature (that it is poor literature in no way changes its status).[4]

This amounts to saying that, once in their final state, the signifier and the signified of fashion clothing do not belong to the same language. This is a crucial distortion, which places fashion within those decoupled, dualized structures that I first tried to describe in a previous essay.[5] Now, the duplicity of the system, set up, as it were, as a halfway house between a language (clothing forms) and a meta-language (the literature of fashion), requires our method to apply a double description: the study of the signifieds (for example of the utopian world they sketch out) is part of a general mythology of fashion. Conversely, the study of the clothing signifiers belongs to a semiological system, in the strict sense of the word. I will leave to one side the former in order to concentrate on the latter; from the signifieds I will retain only their place in the sign.

4. In the majority of other systems of communication, the signifying relation is not given analytically: the system proposes only a chain of signifiers, without *naming* in another way their signifieds: a discourse offers words, not the meaning of each of these words; if the decipherer of a language does not know this language and has no lexicon in it, he [*sic*] has to operate very patiently, by comparing segments in the spoken chain, by moving them around, even in an almost experimental fashion (the commutation test).

With clothing, the autonomy of the signifieds, which are isolated, detached from the signifiers and hoisted to the dizzy heights of fashion literature, constitutes a considerable economy of method. Since its signifiers are given to me with one hand and then the signifieds with the other, it is as if I was being offered, simultaneously, a text and its glossary of words; all I will have to do (in theory) is start from the signs in order to define straightaway the signifiers: defining them is basically to isolate them. If I am told that *blue is in fashion* or that *camellia has the optimistic look about it*, I will come to the conclusion that colour and trimmings are apparently types of signifiers, signifying units.

Then, all I need to do to understand the all-signifying structure of the clothes is look within each unit for those aspects whose opposition helps create meaning (blue/red? blue/white? brooch/flower? camellia/rose?). We will recognize in this schema the two phases of structural analysis: an inventory of the signifying units, and for each unit the setting up of the paradigm of pertinent opposites; the (spatial) syntagmatic division on the one hand, and the construction of a system on the other. I will restrict myself to the first of these, and consider only the inventory that goes with the types of forms.

5. Obviously it is easier to bring into my inventory those links which are entirely verbalized, those links where the signifier is a commentary on the image and not the image itself, because in such links the signified and the signifier belong – at least in the practical sense – to the same language. Unfortunately, the fashion magazine very often gives me links where the signifier is purely graphic (*this* nonchalant ladies' suit, *this* elegant dress, *the* casual two-piece); I then do not have any way – unless intuitively – to decide just what in *this* suit, in *this* dress or in *the* two-piece signifies nonchalance, elegance or casualness: the demonstrative (*this*, *the*)[6] refers here to a general form, and it is this that paradoxically stops me from having any analytical precision without which I cannot isolate the vestimentary sign.

Confronted with these links – what we might call *demonstrative links* – I am a bit like a decipherer who has to uncover the signifying units of a continuous message; the only way here is to look for repetitions: it is by seeing a particular zone of the message coming back, identical to itself, that it can be seen to have the same meaning. Similarly for fashion clothing: it is by looking in a collection of photographs to see how a certain feature goes with the concept of nonchalance that I will finally be able to come to the conclusion that this feature signifies nonchalance – or at least be able to see what I am specially interested in at the moment – that is, whether it really is a unit of meaning.

6. That's one difficulty; here is another one. If I read that *a square-necked, white silk sweater is very smart*, it is impossible for me to say – without again having to revert to intuition – which of these four features (sweater, silk, white, square neck) act as signifiers for the concept *smart*: is it only one feature which carries the meaning, or conversely do non-signifying elements come together and suddenly create meaning as soon as they are combined? Once again here, it will, in theory, be a patient study of the stable residues that will provide me with the answer; or else I will find out that silk, for example, is a material that is necessarily linked to *smartness*, or on the contrary that meaning appears only when, for example, a colour is combined with a material. Either way, it will be useful for me to note that the sweater, silk, white and the squareness of the neck *can* be signifying features; and also to foresee the existence of a fifth,

sufficiently meaningful feature, which is the combination of these four.

7. This example may also be more instructive to me: if by reading other messages I am persuaded that the sweater is very rarely the signifier of the concept *smart* and that the sweater most often imbues the opposite signified (*sport*, for example), I will conclude that the link suggested to me is deliberately paradoxical: a certain number of features (silk, white, square neck) proceed to *undermine* the normal meaning of the sweater. This is a phenomenon of regulation, which is very important in the grammar of fashion. But again what I want to hold on to for the moment is the idea that the sweater is not a signifier here: it is the *object aimed at by meaning*.

In theory we must always be able to define the object that is aimed at in a fashion meaning. This is especially easy in the (fairly rare) cases where meaning acts, so to speak, from a distance, with the feature that carries the meaning being physically separated from the item aimed at. For example, in the following proposition: *patterned blouses give the skirt a touch of romance*, the signifier (*patterned blouses*) is perfectly unconnected with the object aimed at (*the skirt*). In the case of the white silk sweater, the distinction is already more difficult, since the signifiers are in some way incorporated into the item that they signify. In fact, most often the object of meaning is not even referred to; it is the ensemble, the outfit, the grooming, the person in the clothing: since the target is a general one, it is not made precise.

The material element in the link moreover often confuses different functions. When I am told about a *blazer ensemble for cool days*, I am forced to see in the *blazer ensemble* both a signifier and the very object of signification. What's more, this element has a hidden level: it is also the *support* for meaning. This is an important new notion. We can see it clearly in a (rare) example where the three 'levels' are completely detached from one another. Let's say: *a sports cardigan with the collar fastened*. I have three distinct notions here: the object of meaning (this is the cardigan); the support for the meaning (this is the collar); and the signifier proper (this collar is fastened). The supports for meaning take up a lot of space in the fashion lexicon; sometimes, it is true, they are not defined (*blue is in fashion*); but most often, the magazine makes them clear; it has to do this in the numerous cases where meaning comes only from the level of 'detail' (a necklace, the shape of a neckline, the sleeve length, the styling detail, etc.). By definition, the detail is parasitical on the item: the item supports meaning without participating in it, whether it is by 'presenting' it, or by receiving it; the item of clothing is either the object or the support for meaning. Since the support for meaning is more often expressed than the object of meaning, it is the first that needs to be identified, noting meanwhile those rare cases where the support for meaning is different from the object aimed at.

Theoretically speaking, what is a support for meaning? Here we need to think back to language. Language, so it would seem generally, does not have any support for meaning: the word does not *underpin* the meaning, because it *is* the meaning; one cannot abstract the meaning of a word from the (sonorous or written) material which conveys it: it is precisely because structural linguistics has understood this constraint that it has been able to develop at all. However, there is an area where language begins to dualize discourse and transform the verbal chain into a simple support for meaning, an area which I have called elsewhere 'writing' [*l'écriture*]. In literary writing, for example, discourse does have a literal meaning, and in this sense it disallows any dissociation of the object from meaning, and it is a language in the full sense; but this same discourse *supports* a supplementary form of meaning which is not that of the words that it employs, and whose signified is precisely literature: by writing a poem I say certain things, but *at the same time* I point to poetry.

It is roughly the same with fashion clothing, even though literal meaning here is defective in most cases: all that remains is the mythological meaning. In the language of clothing the support for meaning is to all intents and purposes a kind of sign in decline, the inert, domesticated vestige of a world where the sweater would literally signify comfort and warmth, in short the very opposite of *smart*. So it is because fashion clothing is part of a double, unhinged system, where supplementary, secondary meanings rest on initial meanings that are then slowly devitalized, that it involves these supports of meaning that do not exist in single-level semiological analyses.

8. A full link must supply me then with at least three pieces of information: a signifier, a signified and a support for the meaning.

As these links are fairly numerous in fashion magazines, I can risk making a list of them which conforms to the following model:

| Signified: *Five o'clock* | | Signifier(s): *Satin* |
|---|---|---|
| Support for meaning (or object aimed at by it): *A dress* | | |
| Expression of meaning (phraseology): | | *Elle*, no. 611 |
| | 'To give an air of...' | Reference: |

I can classify these data in two ways: by signifieds or by signifiers. This would be a difficult one to choose between if I was dealing with a vast corpus of materials, with statistical importance analogous to that of linguistics, for example.[7] But since the list concerns models that are purely qualitative, it is not difficult for me to try and establish the two sets of classifications. The first will give me all the 'morphemes' of one single signified; I will find out, for example, that the signifiers for 'romantic' are: chiffon, lace, batiste, Swiss cotton, lawn, organza, flounces, hats with veils, headbands; here I am in the same situation as a linguist having to list all the different markers for the plural form (*-s, their*, etc.). But in the same way that the '*s*' is both a marker of the number and of the person (*she sings*),

so organza is the established signifier both for the romantic air
and for the dress to wear to the casino. I am thus referred back to
the context, be it a spatial one (the phrasing or the entire item of
clothing) or an associative one (the oppositions between –'s' and no
's', between, for example, organza and flannel).

It would be better then to put the signifiers into homogenous
classifications, without worrying for the moment about their substance, i.e. their signifieds: the signified will only come back into the
picture with the setting out of the relevant variations within each of
these classifications. What must be distinguished first are the main
generic 'morphemes' of fashion clothing (for which I have reserved
the middle box in my diagram):[8] if I bring together all the signifiers
of the type 'satin', I will quickly find a general 'vesteme': *material*,
inside which I hope to open out, via a series of later studies, an
actual paradigm (whose 'number' I cannot predict)[9] which will contrast in a pertinent way satin with tweed (= morning).

9. For it is the functions that I am trying to highlight. Now, often
the fashion magazine only provides me with a univocal lexicon
(what I will call an *absolute lexicon*), inasmuch as it tends, thanks
to its mythological vocation, to present the signs as unchanging
essences; the magazine will tell me, for example, that *alpaca* means
*summer* or that *lace* means *mystery*, as if it were about 'real' eternal
identities whatever the general spread of other possible meanings:
the more arbitrary its law, the more imperative it is. But I would not
be satisfied with an absolute lexicon that did not allow me to find
the signifying oppositions. The stake is high, because if I am happy
with simple equations (alpaca = summer), I will be induced to make
the meaning into a substance and to lose sight of the mythological
aspect of the signified; whereas, if I manage to disperse fashion's
absolute lexicon across various ranges of relative oppositions, I am
respecting the dualized structure in fashion language, sending the
signified back to its mythological heaven.

10. Fortunately, however, the fashion magazine sometimes aban-
dons the absolute lexicon and itself provides various ranges of oppositions that are all ready set out for me. This is true of what I
will call *concomitant variations of signs*: a change of signified explicitly
brings about a change of signifier, so that I then have at least four
terms (two signifieds and two signifiers), linked to each other by a

kind of proportionality.[10] Let us take the example of *a velvet hat in oatmeal silk* (the support for meaning); for wearing in the *afternoon* (signified no. 1) there are *two straw cabochons* on it (signifier no. 1); for *the evening* (signified no. 2) it has *three jet buttons* (signifier no. 2)

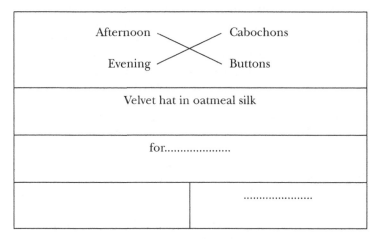

Normally, this variation applies to a contradictory opposition of signifieds (*sensible/ amusing*); but it can also extend to a range of states (*smart/ very smart/ less smart*), of moments (*lunch/ dinner/ cocktail party/ five o'clock tea/ ten o'clock supper*), or of circumstances (*grand ball/ outdoor dance/ private dance/ dance at home*). Here we can see the signifier defining, very closely, a tiny variant of the signified; and we can see gradated signifieds (*more or less smart*) being accompanied by starkly discontinuous signifiers (*dresses with or without their jacket*).

These links are precious because they show in one go the 'vesteme' and its paradigm, showing simultaneously the syntagmatic unit and the systematic opposition that the unit normally implicitly supports. Let's say: a cardigan which is *sporty or casual depending on whether the collar is open or fastened* (the collar is the support for the meaning, the cardigan the object it is aimed at). Not only am I assured immediately that there is a 'vesteme': *the way of wearing an item of clothing* (or, as an abbreviation, the wearing),[11] but also I know that the paradigm implied by this 'vesteme' will include at least the opposition *open/ fastened*.[12]

11. We can make use of these concomitant variations of signs to remind ourselves again of the particular structure of fashion language, of how it resembles articulated language and how it differs from it: articulated language is a single system (unless we consider its stylistic aspects, its *écritures*), fashion clothing is a double system. I will now explain this difference by comparing each of them to a third semiological system, an extremely banal one, but which has the advantage of being either double or single as you wish.

In one part of the highway code I find three signs: red, green, amber. If no one *tells* me what their respective meanings are, I will have to register the real responses to these mysterious stimuli a certain number of times in order to understand that red is 'stop', green is 'go' and amber is 'get ready': here we have a primary system, analogous to articulated language (the message is decoded only by experience). By contrast, if my driving instructor tells me explicitly that red means 'stop', then I have here a secondary system, with spoken language as the relay; however, if the instructor tells me nothing about the other signals (or only tells me later), I will be led to think that red is the *natural*, essential, eternal colour for 'stop'; I will then be absorbing a private meaning artificially detached from any functional structure: this is the case of the *absolute lexicon* (alpaca = summer), which I said represented the normal form of vestimentary communication. But if my instructor explains to me that the three signifieds (stop, go, get ready) are functionally linked to three colours whose difference I only need to observe to understand the message, then I learn a system whose functional structure is finally crystal clear – though this system is also communicated by spoken language: for it will be of little importance (except for the physical reasons of visibility) that the signifying colours are red, green and amber it is purely in the play of their oppositions that I will read the information system offered to me: this is very much the case with my concomitant variations.[13]

12. I am now in a position to propose a first inventory of the homogenous types of clothing signifiers. Each of these types constitutes a kind of syntagmatic unit (what Saussure calls 'concrete units'); they are spatial in nature, 'sections' of clothing. Here is a first list of these types of 'vesteme':

Material
Colour                                          **Details**
Motif                                           Collar
                                                Sleeves
**Items**                                       Pockets
(*defined by their point of support*)           Waist
Head                                            Vents
Neck                                            Fastenings
Shoulders                                       Pleats
Hips                                            Edging
Shoulders–hips (one-piece items)                Stitching
Hands                                           Trimmings
Feet
              Way of wearing
              Association of elements

Naturally, each of these types raises problems, requires explanations. As it is a question here of only outlining a methodological itinerary, I will restrict myself to commenting upon two aspects of this inventory.

13. I will insist again on the following, that these different types do not in any way come from a logical or intuitive consideration of women's clothing. I have not tried to classify the different elements (or features) of this clothing according to the divisions that might be suggested to me by aesthetic, anatomical, technical, commercial, terminological or utilitarian principles: it is simply the signifying power of such and such a zone or accident of clothing which designates them as units, and it is the whole set of morphologically identical units that constitutes a formal type. So it follows that these types are at the same time very near to and a long way off the classification of clothing that common sense might imagine. Very near because – and it is not pointless to restate this in a resolutely 'formalist' investigation – the meanings of (fashion) clothing are obviously linked – *in a certain way*[14] – to a vestimentary practice, to the extent that one finds in clothing as a signifying ensemble the technical matrix to which it is subject (that such and such a stitching is a *sign* does not remove the instrumental function of stitching). And very far off, because an item of clothing (to take the current division of clothes into *articles*)

does not sell according to what it signifies: there are no 'signifiers' on the shelves of large stores.[15] We will get an idea of this ambiguity by considering the very general 'vesteme': the *item* (defined by its point of support).[16] The item and the article do indeed belong to the same order: by definition they are discontinuous objects. But whereas commercial taxonomy distinguishes articles by the complex combination of different criteria (the position on the vertical axis and horizontal axis of the body, the utilitarian function, the shape of the yokes, the existence of a characteristic 'detail', etc.), for the item I do not need to retain that which makes it mean, that which contrasts it with other signifiers: whether by its very existence,[17] or by such and such a detail. It follows then that signifying units are often either bigger or smaller than the commercial article: there can be meaning at the very general level, for example, of the item worn on the outside of the shoulder, be it a coat, cape, raincoat or suit jacket, or simply at the level of a tiny detail (to wear a collar turned up or not); conversely, an article (a jacket, a skirt) can be devoid of all meaning. The first task then for a reading of fashion clothing – also the most intractable, given the commercial nature of the only terminology we have at our disposal – is to break up the notion of article so as to get a grip on the semiogenic element in all its mobility.

14. The second general comment I would like to add to the question of formal types is this: the 'proof' of the vesteme is that it necessarily sits astride two structural planes: that of the syntagm and that of the system. For, on the one hand, the vesteme is indeed a segment of the vestimentary chain, a concrete piece of space, the fragment in a continuum. On the other, if the vesteme occupies this space, it is because it has dislodged, so to speak, all the other concurrent features to which it stands in opposition. To return to the example of the shoulder item, in one way it is a fragment of vestimentary space, in line with the garment worn on the hips, in tune with the other items that have been chosen to be combined with it, to pick up the Hjelmslev-Togeby classification; and all these links of commonality, selection or simple combination are purely syntagmatic: with the point of support and the 'join' in place there can be only one unit of meaning in this body-juncture.[18] In another way, it is actually part of a type: *the shoulder item*; and here a whole

paradigm opens up, in which each term has meaning only because it excludes the others. An *anorak* is a syntagmatic unit in that it links up with a hip item (skirt or trousers); and it is a systemic unit in that it is in opposition to another shoulder item, of a similar sort, such as the *car coat*.[19] So the 'vesteme' always has a double existence: extensive, because it is provided with a concrete (topological) situation; intensive, because it sits at the top of a virtual paradigm of oppositions.

15. The signs I have discussed so far all link to a specific signified: and this is even, I have suggested, to the advantage of fashion clothing in that it supplies its signifieds in the meta-language of a literature. These signifieds are not great in number, and the world they construct is narrow.[20] However, even if we remember that a signified has almost always several signifiers, fashion clothing gives the impression of a surprising flourishing of forms. How can this be?

Here we need to consider a whole set of features for which the fashion magazine does not give the signified, or at least to which it does not attribute an explicit signified: the signified remains, so to speak, 'up in the air'. For example, the simple overall dress will be described to us using a succession of its features (*poplin with white polka dot on Pernod-yellow background, pleated collar and pockets,* etc.), without these features referring to any declared concept: the signified seems to be defective. But this is only in appearance: in all of the cases where the magazine *describes* without commenting, of which there are many, there is always a signified which needs to be added, and this signified is fashion itself;[21] to the extent that these apparently defective equations are full meanings: nothing of what is *said* is insignificant.

Fashion then is a signified like all the others. The only difference is that the other signifieds are episodic and always named. The signified *fashion* is by contrast permanent – it can be found in three forms: explicitly named (*blue is in fashion this year*); supported by contingent signifieds which make up its links (*accessory = spring* {= fashion});[22] or neither named, nor linked, but implicit (*a dress in Pernod poplin*, etc.). It is a universal signified; one could say, to borrow the expression from logic,[23] that in all equations of vestimentary language, whether implicit or not, fashion constitutes the *vector continuum of meaning.*

16. It follows then, that in literary terms, it is within this written meta-language that the fashion magazine supplies its equivalences, and that the signified fashion is supplied using a single signifier, which, both necessary and sufficient, I will call the *notable*: any noted feature, any underlined form, in short any vestimentary fragment points, as soon as it is *cited*, to the signified *fashion*. Therefore I can – and I must – treat all that is *said* by the fashion magazine as a virtual feature of meaning, and make these notations into signifying material and incorporate them into my formal types: moreover they sit here very well, and the list of pure fashion signifiers will coincide pretty closely with the list of more specific signifiers. In this way we are sure of a very wide yet homogenous inventory.

17. Can this inventory (of signifying forms) be exhaustive? It is necessary first to remember that, since the object of this research is purely synchronic, we must have collected only those features and forms found during one year.[24] Furthermore, what is listed are models, not averages; as soon as a feature is recorded, it is no longer necessary to count the number of times it appears: a regular feature is no more meaningful than a rare one; it is not the size of a particular fashion form that allows it to carry meaning, but its relation to other forms.

It follows then, that after a while the inventory of signifying forms will be saturated; in practical terms it never is completely; but if the general structure is established correctly, a form, whatever it is, is never unforeseeable. It is certainly still possible to find a new sign; but if the formal types are well established, it will be incorporated into one or several of these without any friction.

18. For the 'renewal' of fashion is linked essentially to the apparent novelty of combinations, and not to the novelty of features. 'Vestemes' are finite (and probably small) in number[25], and so the total number of their combinations is also; and this total number is even smaller, because certain combinations are impossible by virtue of certain rules of incompatibility. Indeed, the abundance of forms, upon which the whole mythology of fashion is constructed ('caprice', 'taste', 'invention', 'intuition', 'inexhaustible renewal', etc.), is an illusion, which is possible only because, with the synchrony here being very short, the play of combinations easily goes beyond, if only by a little, any human memory of these forms. But all that would be

needed would be to build a mathematical memory (as a machine for making fashion),[26] for fashion to appear, even at the level of a micro-diachrony, to be a limited and essentially computable set of forms: this is a shocking truth for a commerce based entirely on the exaltation of incessant newness, but useful precisely for an understanding of how an ideology *turns* the real *inside out.*

## Notes

1. Published in *Revue Française de Sociologie*, vol. 1 no. 2 (April) 1960, 147–62; *Oeuvres complètes* vol. 1, 856–68.

2. I do not mean here an article of clothing *as it is worn* (even if it is in fashion), but only women's clothing as it is presented in words or in pictures in fashion publications. Such an article of clothing could be defined as a 'utopia'.

3. *Because* is one of fashion literature's favourite conjunctions. There is a curious symmetry between a fashion magazine that tends to convert an equation into a causality, and the way that logic moves in the opposite direction with its refusal to see any truth factors in connectors such as *because* and *in order to*, and its tendency to remove them from logical calculation precisely because, and this is the case of the fashion magazine, these connectors are too empirical. From a purely semiological point of view, the vanity involved in any causal (or final) link between a signifier and a signified is evident in the following (invented) example: think of an advertisement for a make of pipe, with a caption of this sort: 'I am calm, I am strong, I smoke a pipe'. The two inverse causalities have the same impact: I am calm *because* I smoke a pipe; I smoke a pipe *because* I am calm. All we have here is a semantic link.

4. It is true that the signifier is very often communicated via verbal description; but this then is only a substitute for the image (witness the importance of photographs and drawings which the words merely reinforce); whereas the signified *never* exists except in articulated language.

5. *Mythologies*, Paris, Seuil, 1957 [1970].

6. It is obviously not in traditional grammars that you will find demonstratives of this kind listed. You will find a better commentary

in the work by Jacques Damourette and Edouard Pichon (*Essai de grammaire de la langue française*, 1911–1927, Paris, Editions d'Artrey), in the chapter devoted to what the authors call the 'presentational space of the noun' (vol. 1, book 4, ch. VI, 466–518).

7. It is not the same thing to describe a structure according to its signifiers and according to its signifieds. Do the signifiers flow, in some sense genetically, from the signifieds, or conversely is there some endogenous organization of the signifiers? Benoît Mandelbrot has asked this question remarkably in L. Apostel, B. Mandelbrot and A. Morf, *Logique, langage et théorie de l'information*, Paris, PUF, 1957, p. 63 [and *passim*; Mandelbrot reiterates Saussure's point that, if the former pertains then semiology will be tied to other forms of enquiry; if the latter pertains, then semiology, as the study of signifiers on their own, will be independent of other sciences, which, argues Mandelbrot, is what Saussure wanted].

8. For these vestimentary morphemes I propose the noun 'vestemes', by analogy to Claude Lévi-Strauss's 'mythemes'.

9. Not having yet completed the inventory of oppositions, I still do not know if these are binary or complex.

10. Proportionality is a notion which is not very compatible with the discontinuous nature of signifiers; but the signifieds, for their part, are often quantified: *ensembles that are more or less smart, more and more fantasy*, etc.

11. The way of wearing an item can be put on a structural inventory only if this way of wearing is institutionalized: here we have the Saussurian distinction between *langue* and *parole*; just as linguistics is interested only in phenomena of *langue*, so a semiology of clothing only retains normative features. And indeed fashion clothing has the methodological advantage of being institutional clothing in its pure state – because it is not worn.

12. We can already predict a neutral term for this opposition (neither open, nor fastened), which (on certain overcoats) is edge to edge [*bord à bord*]. But since the edge to edge is found in the opposition *edge to edge wrapped around*, we would then have a function with four terms: *wrapped around/ fastened/ open/ edge to edge*.

13. To what extent is green the *opposite* of red? One might say that the existence of a third term or neutral term (neither red, nor green) reinforces the polarity between the first two.

14. The link between the technical matrices of clothing and the organization of its signifiers goes back to the problem set out in note 7 above.

15. There would be some interest in comparing how a catalogue for a large store organizes the fashion signifiers and the classification of articles for clothing. The problem of these taxonomies has been taken up by Mandelbrot (*Logique, langage et théorie de l'information*, Paris, PUF, 1957, p. 57) following George Kingsley Zipf, *Human Behaviour and the Principle of Least Effort*, Cambridge, Mass., Addison Wesley editions, 1949 and Gustav Herdan, *Language as Choice and Change*, Groningen, P. Noordhof N.V., 1956.

16. The criterion *point of support* with which to define an item comes from ethnology (André Leroi-Gourhan, *Milieu et techniques*, p. 208 [see also note 6 in chapter 3 here, 'Towards Sociology of Dress']). This does not stop it coinciding with the criterion of meaning, except for a few things that are limited to Western clothing.

17. On the level of item we could suggest an opposition: *presence, absence*. Let 'E' be the item for the shoulders; in certain conditions 'E+'(women) 'E−'(men).

18. One of the difficulties in the structural analysis of clothing is its two-dimensional nature. Clothing items are to be found on both the horizontal and the vertical axis, as they layer themselves on top of each other in thickness and in height. I have decided to call the vertical superposing of items 'strata' (e.g. hat, scarf, jacket, skirt, shoes), and their horizontal superposing 'layers' (e.g. for men, vest, shirt, jacket, coat). Of course, the 'strata' have a much greater semantic importance than the 'joins' because semiology by definition is interested in the visible. The problem becomes complicated when, firstly, certain joins are partially visible (the collar part of the shirt); and secondly when the joins are not stable (which shows how necessary it is to distinguish the article from the item): a jacket can be an external or an internal item (under a coat). However, an item is defined entirely by the stratum (point of support) to which it belongs, and by the join of which it is a part (internal, external, mixed).

19. [Editors' note: 'car coat' is a woman's coat worn in the 1950s in the car in France, across the shoulders, rather like a trench coat. We are grateful to Bruno Remaury for this clarification.]

20. The signifieds probably organize themselves into the main functions of the following type: town/country, smart/sporty, daytime/evening, etc.

21. Of course, fashion must always be understood in its temporal sense: *blazer* = spring, *this year*.

22. In a more restricted sense a 'psychological' signified can itself be a link for a circumstantial signified, such as *coat* = *travel*, via the intermediary of the signified: *comfortable*.

23. Robert Blanché, *Introduction à logique contemporaine*, Paris, A. Colin, 1950, p.138.

24. In between a strict synchrony (fashion over one year) and a wide diachrony, as studied by Richardson and Kroeber, there is space for a micro-diachrony which would try to structure the variations of one 'vesteme' over several years; for example, skirt length. This micro-diachrony is possible because fashion signifiers depend on rules and not on usage (the opposite of language).

25. I repeat: I have treated types of 'vestemes', not 'vestemes' themselves, the inventory for which needs a systematic analysis.

26. If it is true that a fashion *line* comes from treating a certain number of 'vestemes', then it is close, in cybernetic terms, to the machine as *idea*, 'a long calculation on a series of different operations (phonemes)' (Mandelbrot, *Logique, langage et théorie de l'information*, Paris, PUF. 1957, p. 44) [Mandelbrot asks us to consider the very limited number of operations in a machine as its 'phonemes', and the long calculation it is asked to do as an idea; thus the phonemes must represent, slowly, the 'idea' that they are to communicate. It is clearly useful for Barthes to see this linguistic analogy being used in another science, here logic and cybernetics].

# 5

# From Gemstones to Jewellery[1]

For a long time, for centuries, perhaps even millennia, the gemstone was considered to be essentially a mineral substance; whether it was diamond or metal, precious stone or gold, it always came from the earth's depths, from that sombre and fiery core, of which we see only the hardened and cooled products; in short, by its very origin, the gemstone was an infernal object that had come through arduous, often bloody journeys, to leave behind those subterranean caverns where humanity's mythic imagination stored its dead, its damned and its treasures in the same place.

Extracted from hell, the gemstone came to symbolize hell, and took on its fundamental characteristic: the inhuman. Like stone (and stones provided a large amount of gems), it was associated above all with hardness: stone has always stood for the very essence of things, for the irremediably inanimate object; stone is neither life nor death, it represents the inert, the stubbornness of the thing to be nothing but itself; it is the infinitely unchanging. It follows then, that stone is pitiless; whereas fire is cruel, and water crafty, stone is the despair of that which has never lived and will never do so, of that which obstinately resists all forms of life. Through the ages the gemstone extracted from its mineral origins its primary symbolic power: that of announcing an order as inflexible as that of things.

Nevertheless, humanity's poetic imagination was able to conceive of stones that were made to wear out, noble, venerable stones, which grew old and so were, despite everything, alive. As for the quintessential stone, the diamond, it is beyond time: never wearing, incorruptible, its limpidness forms the moral image of the most deadly of virtues – purity; in terms of substance, the diamond is pure, clean, almost aseptic; but whereas there are some purities that are tender, fragile (water for example), there are others that are sterile, cold, steely; for purity is life, but it can also be, by contrast, infertility, and the diamond is like the sterile son emerging from the deepest point of the earth, non-productive, incapable of rotting down, hence incapable of becoming the source of new life.

And yet, it seduces; hard and limpid, the diamond has a third symbolic quality: it glistens. Here it is incorporated into a new magical and poetic domain, that of the paradoxical substance, both lit up and stone cold: it is nothing but fire and yet nothing but ice. This cold fire, this sharp, shining object which is nevertheless silent, what a symbol for the whole world of vanities, of seductions devoid of content, of pleasures devoid of sincerity! For centuries, Christian humanity felt deeply (much more than we do today) the opposition between the world and solitude; thanks to its fire-like sparkle and its coldness, the diamond was this world, this abhorrent and fascinating order of ambition, flattery and disappointment, condemned by so many of our moralists – perhaps in order better to describe it.

And what about gold, which was also used to make gemstones? Though originating in the earth and in hell, arriving first as ore or as nugget, gold is a substance more intellectual than symbolic; it holds a fascination only within certain mercantile economies; it has no, or very little, poetic reality; it is only ever mentioned so as to show how this most mediocre of substances (a dull, yellowy metal) clashes with the importance of its effects. But as a sign, what power it has! And it is precisely the sign par excellence, the sign of all the signs; it is absolute value, invested with all powers including those once held by magic: is it not able to appropriate *everything*, goods and virtues, lives and bodies? Is it not able to convert *everything* into its opposite, to lower and to elevate, to demean and to glorify? The gemstone has long participated in this power of gold. And this is not all: owing to the fact that gold very quickly stopped being convertible or useful and so removed itself from any practical application, pure gold, whose usefulness was almost entirely self-referential, became superlative gold, absolute richness – here the gemstone becomes the very concept of *price*; it is worn like an idea, that of a terrific power, for it is enough to be seen for this power to be demonstrated.

There is no doubt that, fundamentally, the gemstone was a sign of superpower, that is of virility, and remained so for a very long time (after all, it is only recently and under the puritan influence of

Quaker clothing, which is the origin of men's clothing today, that men stopped wearing gemstones). So why in our world has it been associated so constantly with woman, with her powers and her evil spells? It is because the husband very quickly delegated to his wife the job of showing off his own wealth (certain sociologists use this to explain the origins of fashion): the wife provides poetic proof of the wealth and power of the husband. Except that, as always with human society, a simple pattern is quickly invested with unexpected meanings, symbols and effects. Thus the primitive showing-off of wealth has been invaded by a whole mythology of woman: this mythology remains infernal, because woman would give everything to own gemstones, and man would give everything to own that very woman who wears the gemstones that she has sold herself for; with gemstones as the link, woman gives herself up to the Devil, the husband to the woman, who has herself become a precious, hard stone; and we must not assume that a symbolism of this sort, which is both prosaic, spiritual and, after all, naive, belongs only to the barbarous periods in Western history. The whole of the Second Empire in France (1852–1871) for example was intoxicated and panic-stricken by the power of gemstones, by this capacity to *induce* human Evil, which for so long had been almost a physical property of diamond and gold: Zola's *Nana* really is the grandiose and angry cry of a society destroying itself, or one might even say devouring itself, in two ways; woman is both a man-eater and a diamond-eater.

Such a mythology has not completely disappeared from our times: there are still fine jewellers, a world market in diamonds and thefts of famous gemstones. But their infernal aspect is clearly on the decline. First, because the mythology of woman has changed: in the novel, in films, woman is less and less the femme fatale, no longer the destroyer of men; she can no longer be essentialized, stopped from existing or made into a precious and dangerous object; she has rejoined the human race. And also gemstones, the great mythical gemstones, are barely worn nowadays; they are of historical value only, sterilized, embalmed and kept away from the female body, condemned to sit in a safe. In short, fashion – need I say more? – no longer speaks of the gemstone but only of jewellery.

Now fashion, as we know, is a language: through it, through the system of signs it sets up, no matter how fragile this may seem, our society – and not just that of women – exhibits, communicates its being, says what it thinks of the world; so, just as the gemstone basically expressed the essentially theological nature of ancient society, so jewellery today, as seen in shops and in fashion magazines, merely follows, expresses and signifies our times – having originated in the ancestral world of the damned, the piece of jewellery has in one word become *secularized*.

First and foremost this secularization has visibly affected the very substance of jewellery; it is no longer made from just stone or metal, but also fragile or soft materials such as glass or wood. Furthermore, jewellery is no longer routinely given the job of showing off a prize that is, so to speak, inhuman: you see jewellery made of common metal, of inexpensive glass; and when jewellery imitates some precious substance, gold or pearls, it is shameless; the copy, now a characteristic of capitalist civilization, is no longer a hypocritical way of being rich on the cheap – it is quite open about itself, makes no attempt to deceive, only retaining the aesthetic qualities of the material it is imitating. In short, there has been a widespread liberation of jewellery; its definition is widening, it is now an object that is free, if one can say this, from prejudice: multiform, multi-substance, to be used in an infinite variety of ways, it is now no longer subservient to the law of the highest price nor to that of being used in only one way, such as for a party or sacred occasion: jewellery has become democratic.

Of course, this democratization does not escape from new ways of conferring value. As long as wealth regulated the rarity of a gemstone, the latter could be judged by nothing but its price (that of its substance and of the work put into it); but once just about anyone could procure whatever they wanted, as soon as the work of art became a product, there had to be a way, in our democratic, but still differentiated, societies, of subjecting jewellery to another form of discrimination: and this is *taste*, of which fashion is precisely the judge and the keeper. So today we have *jewellery of bad taste*; and, rather paradoxically, what defines bad taste in a piece of jewellery is curiously that which was once the very sign of its prestige and of its magical qualities: namely its highest price; not only is jewellery that is too rich or too heavy now discredited but conversely, for expensive jewellery to have good taste, its richness must be discreet, sober, visible certainly but only to those in the know.

So what counts as good taste in jewellery today? Quite simply this: no matter how little it costs, the piece of jewellery must be thought about in relation to the whole outfit it accompanies, it must be subjected to that essentially functional value which is that of style. What is new, if you like, is that the piece of jewellery is no longer on its own; it is one term in a set of links that goes from the body to clothing, to the accessory and includes the circumstances for which the whole outfit is being worn; it is part of an ensemble, and this ensemble is no longer necessarily ceremonial: taste can be everywhere, at work, in the country, in the morning, in winter, and the piece of jewellery follows suit; it is no longer a singular, dazzling, magical object, conceived as a way of ornamenting and thus making woman *look her best*; it is now more humble and more active, an element of clothing which enters into an equal relationship with a material, with a particular cut or with another accessory.

So it is precisely its smallness, its finished look, its very substance as the opposite of the fluidity of fabrics, that makes the piece of jewellery part of fashion and it has become almost like the soul in the general economy of clothing: that is, *the detail*. It was inevitable that, in making taste into the product of a subtle set of functions, fashion would give more and more weight to the simple presence of one element, no matter how small and without regard for its physical importance; this gives rise to the highest value in today's fashion being placed on anything insignificant in size but which is able to modify, harmonize, animate the structure of a set of clothes, and it is called precisely (but from now on with a lot of respect) a *next-to-nothing*. The piece of jewellery is a *next-to-nothing*, but out of this next-to-nothing comes great energy. Often inexpensive, sold in simple 'boutiques' and no longer in the temples of jeweller's shops, available in a variety of materials, free in its styles (often including the exotic even), in short *depreciated* in the true sense of the word, in its physical state, the most modest piece of jewellery remains the vital element in getting dressed, because it underlines the desire for order, for composition, for intelligence. Analogous to those half-chemical, half-magical, substances which act all the more forcefully by virtue of their infinitesimal size, the piece of jewellery *reigns* over clothing not because it is absolutely precious but because it plays a crucial role in making clothing mean something. It is the *meaning* in a style which now becomes precious and this meaning depends, not on each element, but on the link between them and in this link it is the *detached* term (a pocket, a flower, a scarf, a piece of jewellery) that holds the ultimate power of signification. This is a truth that is not only analytical but also poetic: this great journey across centuries and across societies, from the gemstone to jewellery, is the very same itinerary that has transformed the cold and luxurious stones in the Baudelairian universe into those trinkets, pieces of jewellery and next-to-nothings in which Mallarmé could then enclose a whole metaphysics of the new power of Man to make the tiniest of things have meaning.

## *Note*

1. Published in *Jardin des Arts*, 77 (April), 1961; *Oeuvres complètes* vol. 1, 911–14.

# 6

# *Dandyism and Fashion*[1]

For centuries there were as many clothing items as there were social classes. Every social condition had its garment and there was no embarrassment in making an outfit into a veritable sign, since the gap between the classes was itself considered to be natural. So, on the one hand, clothing was subject to an entirely conventional code, but on the other, this code referred to a natural order, or even better to a divine order. To change clothes was to change both one's being and one's social class, since they were part and parcel of the same thing. So we see in Marivaux's plays, for example, the game of love getting caught in mix-ups over identities, in the possible permutations of social standing and in the swapping of clothes. There was at this time a true grammar of clothing, something that was not simply a question of taste, and which one could not transgress without affecting the deeper organization of the world: how many plots and intrigues in our classical literature rely on the clearly signalled characteristics of clothing!

We know that in the aftermath of the French Revolution men's clothing changed drastically, not only in its form (which came essentially from the Quaker model), but also in its spirit: the idea of democracy produced a form of clothing which was, in theory, uniform, no longer subject to the stated requirements of *appearances* but to those of work and equality. Modern clothing (for our men's clothing is largely that of the nineteenth century) is, in theory, both practical and dignified: it has to be adaptable to any work situation (provided that it is not manual work); and with its austere, or at least sober, form, it must signal that moral *cant* which characterized the bourgeoisie of the last century.

In fact, the separation of the social classes was not abolished at all: though defeated politically, the aristocrat still maintained a powerful prestige, albeit one limited to lifestyle; and the bourgeois man also had to defend himself, not against the worker (whose clothing remained clearly marked), but against the rise of the middle classes. So clothing had to cheat, as it were, the theoretical uniformity that the Revolution and Empire had bequeathed it; and within a universal type of clothing, there was now a need to maintain a certain number of formal differences which could exhibit the difference between social classes.

It is here that we see the appearance of a new aesthetic category in clothing, destined for a long future (women's clothing today is very fond of this, as a cursory glance in any fashion magazine will show): the *detail*. Since it was no longer possible to change the basic type of clothing for men without affecting the democratic and work ethos, it was the *detail* (the 'next-to-nothing', the 'je ne sais quoi', the 'manner', etc.) which started to play the distinguishing role in clothing: the knot on a cravat, the material of a shirt, the buttons on a waistcoat, the buckle on a shoe, were from then on enough to highlight the narrowest of social differences. At the same time, the superiority of status, which for democratic reasons could no longer be advertised, was hidden and sublimated beneath a new value: *taste*, or better still, as the word is appropriately ambiguous, *distinction*.

A distinguished man is a man who marks himself off from the crowd using modest means, but it is a means whose power, which is a kind of energy, is immense. Since, on the one hand, his aim is to be recognized only by his peers, and on the other, this recognition relies essentially on details, the distinguished man adds to the uniform of his century a number of *discreet* signs (that is, those that are both barely visible and yet not in keeping with the outfit), which are no longer spectacular signs of a condition that is openly adopted but the simple signs of a tacit agreement. Indeed, *distinction* takes the signalling aspect of clothes down a semi-clandestine path: for, on the one hand, the group that reads its signs is a limited one, on the other the signs necessary for this reading are rare and, without a particular knowledge of the new vestimentary language, perceptible only with difficulty.

The dandy (and we are talking only about his clothing, as we know that dandyism is more than simply vestimentary behaviour) is a man who has decided to radicalize the distinction in men's clothing by subjecting it to an absolute logic. Furthermore, he takes distinction that bit further: its essence is no longer social for him, but metaphysical; the dandy stands in opposition not at all to the upper class and the lower class, but only in absolute terms to the individual and the banal; so the individual is not a generalized idea for him; it is him alone, purified of all recourse to comparison, to the extent even that, like Narcissus, it is to himself and him alone that he offers a reading of his clothing. Furthermore he professes that its essence, like that of the gods, can be fully present in what is the slightest of elements: the vestimentary 'detail' is no longer a concrete object here, no matter how minute; it is a way, often subtly indirect, of destroying or 'deforming' clothing, of removing it from all sense of value as soon as a value becomes a shared one; it involves making the valet wear a new outfit, making his gloves wet so that they fit the shape of the hand perfectly, all forms of behaviour which bear witness to the profoundly creative, and no longer simply selective, idea that the *effects* of a form have to be thought through, that clothing is not simply an object to be used but is a prepared *object*.

Dandyism therefore is not only an ethos (on which much has been written since Baudelaire and Barbey) but also a technique. It is these two together which make a dandy, and it is obviously the latter which guarantees the former, as with all *ascetic* philosophies (of the Hindu type, for example) in which a physical form of behaviour acts as a route towards the performance of thought; and since this thought consists here of an absolutely singular vision of self, the dandy is condemned to invent continually distinctive traits that are ever novel: sometimes he relies on wealth to distance himself from the poor, other times he wants his clothes to look worn out to distance himself from the rich – this is precisely the job of the 'detail' which is to allow the dandy to escape the masses and never to be engulfed by them; his singularity is absolute in essence, but limited in substance, as he must never fall into eccentricity, for that is an eminently copyable form.

The 'detail' allowed his clothing, in theory, to become indefinitely 'other'. In fact, the ways of wearing an item of clothing are very limited and if certain details in manufacture do not intervene, any renewal of an outfit is quickly exhausted. This is what happened when men's clothing was fully industrialized: deprived of any artisanal manufacture, the dandy had to give up on any absolutely singular form of clothing, for as soon as a form is standardized, even with luxury clothing, it can no longer ever be unique. So ready-to-wear clothing was the first fatal setback for dandyism. But, more subtly, what ruined dandyism for good, was the birth of 'original' boutiques; these boutiques sold clothes and accessories which were not part of mass culture; but because this exclusivity was part of commerce, albeit within the luxury sector, it became itself normative: by buying a shirt, a tie or cufflinks at X or at Z, one was *conforming* to a certain style, and abdicating all personal (one might say narcissistic) invention of singularity. However, it was fundamental to dandyism to be creative, the dandy would *conceive* his outfit exactly like a modern artist might conceive a composition using available materials (such as pieces of paper stuck together); that is, it was normally impossible for a dandy to *purchase* his clothes. But once limited to the freedom to buy (but not to create), dandyism could not but suffocate and die; buying the latest Italian shoes or English tweed is now a very common thing to do in that it is a conformity to Fashion.

Indeed, Fashion is the collective imitation of regular novelty; even when it has the alibi of individual expression, or, as we say today, of a 'personality', it is essentially a mass phenomenon in which sociologists are very happy to be interested so long as they find in it the privileged example of a completely pure dialectic between the individual and society. Furthermore, Fashion has today become everybody's business as shown by the extraordinary growth of women's publications specializing in this area. Fashion is an institution and today nobody believes any more that it *distinguishes*; only *unfashionable* is a notion of distinction; in other words, in terms of the masses Fashion is only ever perceived via its opposite: Fashion is health, it is a moral code of which the unfashionable is nothing but illness or perversion.

So we have witnessed the following paradox: Fashion has exterminated all *considered* singularity in clothing by tyrannically appropriating its institutional singularity. It is not the clothing item itself which has become bureaucratized (for example in societies without fashion), but more subtly its aim towards singularity. To inoculate all of contemporary clothing, via Fashion, with a bit of dandyism was always going to kill dandyism itself since, in its very essence, dandyism was condemned to be radical or not exist at all. It is not therefore the general socialization of the world which has killed dandyism (as one might imagine in a society with rigorously uniform clothing, such as Chinese society today); it was the intervention of an intermediary power between the absolute individual and the total mass of society: Fashion has in some way been given the job of making more subtle and of neutralizing dandyism; modern democratic society has made fashion into a sort of cross-subsidizing organism, destined to establish an automatic equilibrium between the demand for singularity and the right for all to have it. There is clearly a contradiction in terms here: society has made fashion viable only by subjecting vestimentary innovation to a strictly regular duration, slow enough for one to be able to be subject to it, but fast enough to initiate buying rhythms and to establish a distinction of fortunes between men.

It seems that, for women's clothing, the high number of elements (we might say *units*) of which fashion is made up still allows for a rich set of possible combinations and consequently for an authentic individuation of an outfit. But we have seen, without talking about the psychological traits (probably narcissistic and homosexual) which have made dandyism into an essentially masculine phenomenon, that dandy clothing was possible only during this historically ephemeral period when clothing was uniform in its type and variable in its details. Though slower and less radical than women's fashion, men's does none the less exhaust the variation in details, yet without, for many years, touching any aspect of the fundamental type of clothing: so Fashion, then, deprives dandyism of both its limits and its main source of inspiration – it really is Fashion that has killed dandyism.

## Note

1. Published in *United States Lines Paris Review,* special number on Dandyism, July 1962; *Oeuvres complètes* vol. 1, 963–66.

# 7

# *[An Early Preface to]* The Fashion System[1]

Without wishing to associate them inconsiderately with the errors in a work in which they are not involved, I would nonetheless like to thank for their support, advice and friendship, which allowed me to complete this study: Fernand Braudel, G. Friedmann, Cl. Lévi-Strauss, Jean Stoetzel, G. Greimas, Henri Raymond, Marthe Robert and Jean Vannier.

## *Preface*

The object of this study is not a sociology, or a psychology, nor an aesthetics, and even less so a philosophy of Fashion;[2] but something, unfortunately, much drier; for the aim here is above all method-ological. What we wanted expressly to do here was to apply the analytical procedures of structural linguistics to a non-linguistic object, Fashion clothing, and thereby reconstitute the formal system of meaning which humans elaborate using this object;[3] in short, if a little approximate, to establish a 'grammar' of Fashion. In other words, this work can be defined as an attempt at applied *semiology*.

Fifty years ago, in his *Course on General Linguistics*, Saussure postul-ated the birth and the development of a general science of signs, which he called *Semiology*, of which linguistics was to be but a part, albeit an exemplary one. Initially taken up here and there in the work of Saussurian-influenced structural linguistics, the semiological project has very recently enjoyed a much wider currency from the moment when a whole series of different research activities, which had commenced independently, all matured at the same time and converged towards a new epistemological complex, consisting of information theory, formal logic and linguistics, and concerned with the analysis of systems of meaning. It is still far too early to write the history of this new current; many filiations can be found in it that probably go beyond Saussure himself, not to mention those *orthogenetic* phenomena which show that the same idea can appear at the same time in different authors. However, it is when a methodological intention mushrooms outside its original idea that its unifying principle is revealed: by treating a set of ethnological objects persistently in terms of meaning (kinship relations, myths, totemic representations), Cl. Lévi-Strauss has opened up the social sciences to the idea of semiology (often confused with the idea of structural analysis thanks to Saussurian linguistics); and if the investigations of Jean-Claude Gardin and those of Lacan remain rather specialized in the former's drawing up of inventories and in the latter's being deliberately ambiguous,[4] they are nonetheless (to limit ourselves to the French domain) a part of semiology's currency in the way in which they link the human psyche and a large part of world memory to this new science of signs. The present work is undoubtedly aiming quite deliberately to be part of this movement; but, compared to the intensity of the work being undertaken in this area at the moment, our work may appear to be lagging somewhat.[5] First, because our work had already started about seven years ago (though unfortunately this delay does not explain the precarious nature of the results presented here), and because the very principle of this study required a logical rather than a syncretic impetus and was not primarily concerned with the development of semiological theory. And most importantly because we wanted continually to return this study to its primary objective, which was to apply the semiological analysis postulated by Saussure to a non-linguistic object, Fashion clothing; this explains why we had to refrain from taking part in the semiological debate, for example by arguing for semiology's pertinence on the one hand, and for that of the social sciences on the other (not to mention that of Marxism, psychoanalysis and phenomenology), but also why we wanted obstinately and narrowly to consider methodically, step by step and in a literal fashion, a particular method of analysis and a particular object. In short, this book [*The Fashion System*] is an *exercise*, and thus only indirectly part of semiology's current usage (which is actually somewhat Borgesian in the manner in which semiological discourse is infinite whilst its object infinitely delayed); so one should not expect to find any more or less of a link here between this work and the current close reflections on semiology than, say, between a collection of musical scales and the theory of tonality. On the other hand, however, inasmuch as it is – arguably – linked to structuralism, semiology is nevertheless far from being a recognized (or even known) science and how could it be, since it does not exist? The lateness with which our work here is appearing cannot fail to be augmented paradoxically by an esoteric element: that is both its banality and its provocative nature, such is the uncomfortable situation in relation to the historical moment in which this work finds itself.

Like all objects, fashion clothing (that is, women's clothes as described by Fashion every year in its specialist publications) can be studied from several points of view. We can analyse the way in which the clothing is manufactured (technology), launched on to the market (economics), or disseminated into real society (sociology); we can reconstruct its history, its aesthetics or its psychology. None of these points of view is exclusive but each requires a particular method in the sense that each analysis retains only certain aspects of Fashion clothing, depending on what the initial aim is: the technician will see in fashion clothing only what has brought about its fabrication; the economist prices, the sociologist the clothing models, the historian how things have changed, the aesthetician the forms, the psychologist attitudes; and it is by starting from these chosen traits that each analysis will be built; in other words, each one isolates in the object of study 'a homogenous level of description' dependent on the set of aspects which are of interest to the point of view adopted, which means of course that the rest are wilfully discarded. This choice – augmented necessarily by an act of rejection – is called *pertinence* by linguists; 'pertinent' means all those traits of the object that can be apprehended by the point of view which the analyst has decided to adopt. The pertinence principle, well formulated by André Martinet[6] but whose epistemological importance is yet to be measured, dominates entirely (at least it is hoped) the work presented here; confronted with fashion clothing we have chosen, from the outset, 'an homogenous level of description', to which we have tried to hold as rigorously as possible; the pertinence chosen is that of semantics;[7] we have decided to look at contemporary Fashion clothing *from the point of view of the meanings that society attributes to it*, to the exclusion of all other points of view.[8]

Pertinence is at first glance a costly operation since the analysis which accompanies it has to exclude from the phenomenon studied a large number of factors which seem quite reasonably to be crucial parts of it: for example, we are taking Fashion here as if this institution, whose signifying element alone we are considering, lived free of charge amongst humans and without any economic, sociological, or historical basis. Everyone knows however that the Fashion phenomenon is linked to a certain economic gap within societies, characterized generally by the need to sell an object (clothing) at a rate which is faster than its wearing out; and that in the renewal of Fashion models, in their organization and dissemination, there intervene elements for which psychosociology alone can account;[9] and, if the contents of Fashion cannot be directly attached to the contents of history at the level of event, as Kroeber and Richardson have shown, then the phenomenon itself could not be explained except by recourse to a specifically historical, mental category: there is a definite link between Fashion and history at the structural level. By overlooking these categorically fundamental determinations (and considered fundamental especially today), semantic pertinence seems to be undermining the most arrogant of explanatory principles in contemporary social sciences: the principle of totality.

However, it appears that in applied research the totality principle has a fairly low level of payback; either it remains theoretical (as in the sociology of G. Gurvitch) or else, whilst claiming a totality, research in fact is beholden to a particular pertinence (socioeconomic, phenomenological or psychoanalytical); and so the desire to exorcise the myth of determinism in recent years has been a very pious one. So it is better then not to set totality directly in opposition to the pertinence principle and to let this principle develop freely with all these consequences: perhaps then we will see that it is less costly than one thought and that it has a better chance of returning, in its own way, to the totality of a phenomenon than if it performed its analysis, in however voluntary a way, from a single point of view.

Whilst accepting to coexist with other pertinences, semiology (for that is the particular pertinence under discussion here) does not aim to be a partial form of analysis; in its own way it tends towards a certain norm of totality. On the one hand, it tries to include the largest section possible of the real in its description; although by being systematic it cannot be exhaustive, because every system is in its way total, it nevertheless tends ceaselessly to recover a real which is called something different by other pertinences; for example, aesthetic notions like taste or elegance can have their semiological equivalent. On the other hand, it always forces itself to highlight the points in its own system where it uses other pertinences and it actively recognizes the points of crossover and defection in its object of study; whilst working on meaning, it is part of its project to indicate, for example, where meaning ends and where economy, art and the psyche begin. Furthermore, though we have not allowed ourselves to step outside semantic pertinence and as a consequence we should not expect to discover any 'idea' on the philosophy of clothes in this research, we have nevertheless been constantly mindful to point out, as we go along, that there are moments in semiological analysis when we could insert and develop analyses that work with a different pertinence: the semiology of Fashion necessarily contains a certain number of 'doors' leading, for example, to a sociology or a psychology of clothing; and whilst we have stopped ourselves going through these doors, we have made sure that they are pointed out – in the same way that phonology, though constituting a closed pertinence, recognizes the (physical) reality of those articulated sounds that it studies only from the point of view of meaning. Are we talking about an epistemological liberalism here? Not exactly: neither totalizing, nor partial, semiology can handle this contradiction quite naturally, in that it is nothing but a *language*, merely a particular way of talking about Fashion clothing. On the one hand, semiology sees itself as a complete language, sufficiently wide so as to be coherent (so it is not an analysis of little bits), but on the other it is happy for other languages to work on the same object (so it is not a dogmatic analysis); this double attitude in fact depends on the idea that Science is never completely the pure real nor pure language.[10] As language, semiological pertinence has to be exhaustive (inasmuch as every system is exhaustive); but as the real, the object that it focuses on escapes from it at a certain moment to go towards other languages (which of course do not have a monopoly on totality any more than it does). In other words, the pertinence principle appears inevitable from the moment when we refuse to conflate, in absolute terms, language and the real and when we see that the link which unites the one to the other is one of validity and not one of truth. The application of pertinence then has nothing to do with scientist 'rigour' (with carefully delimiting the object in order to study it in all 'modesty' and 'objectivity'), but corresponds rather to a reaction against a certain positivism in the social sciences, when they refuse to recognize in their analyses of the real the distant nature of their own language, no matter how 'banal'.

Furthermore (and this is its second advantage) the pertinence principle, though a guide for focused work on a very specific object, allows for a better knowledge of the whole set of processes of meaning. Certainly these processes are now well elucidated in terms of articulated language.[11] But what about the other systems, made up of objects whose original existence is not that of signification, but to which the social human being (that belonging precisely to sociology) gives new meanings? What happens within a collection of objects, when humans decide to give it the task of transmitting meaning? How does the collection become *system* (outside which there could be no communication)? How does meaning come to humans? This question, which defines semiology, needs two replies, one intensive, the other extensive. With regard to the former, we need on the one hand to tackle once and for all that very structure of an object that is independent of language, and it is contemporariness itself which requires this: these days there is a constant use made of the concepts of meaning which are applied to all sorts of objects and phenomena; be it concessions to fashion in vocabulary, or recourse to a new word which is aimed at replacing nominally the old determinist schema, there is nothing today, from the cinema to the machine, which is not deemed 'language'. However, calling these phenomena 'language' is still to remain purely at the level of metaphor; for what makes something language is not the *expression* of a certain immateriality by a certain materiality but the existence of a differential system of discontinuous units; this is to the extent that, for each of the phenomena considered, no one has been able to establish an exhaustive system and thus the concepts of meaning and of language remain hypothetical or metaphorical; so, by engaging in the setting up of a semantic system for an object like clothing, we wanted to observe in all its minuteness the way in which meaning functions within an object (clothing), about which it has often been said that it is a language[12] but without this ever having been demonstrated: in short, given the metaphorical abuse of the word and the price we pay for this (we are thinking of the inevitable promotion of a certain formalism), it was finally time to enter (so to speak) into the kitchen of meaning. And on the other hand, this thorough exploration of the inside of a particular object (here Fashion clothing) should serve as a model for a series of similar explorations inside other objects with semiology not being able to operate fully until all systems of signification be defined by their differences and their residual commonality.[13] Then, by extension, major objects in mass culture (to remain within the sociological field) would then need to be listed, from food to journalistic narrative; but the analysis of the Fashion system, whatever the imperfections and gaps, will perhaps already be able to supply a few operational models.

Finally, as a semantic object, Fashion clothing has a fundamental link to what is generally called *global society* in that to practise semiological analysis, however narrowly focused, is to rediscover this society in all its anthropological generality. But to uncover this link, we must – paradoxically – accept that sociology and semiology, though starting with the same object, namely Fashion, develop in two entirely different directions. The sociology of Fashion starts out with a *model* that is imaginary in origin (clothing conceived by the *fashion-group*), and then continues to completion (or at least *will* continue, the day it comes into existence) by using a series of *real* clothes (this is the problem for the dissemination of clothing models); and therefore sociology aims to systematize behaviours which it can easily link to social conditions, living standards and collective attitudes. Semiology does not go down the same road at all; it describes an article of clothing which remains imaginary, or if you like, purely intellective, which leads to an identification not of practices but of images. The sociology of Fashion is tuned entirely to a sociology of real clothing; the semiology of fashion to a sociology of representations; semiology's horizon is not real clothing but ideology in general and within this horizon the Fashion object slowly dissolves to reveal a global phenomenon par excellence: the human *intelligible*. It is not simply via (or starting from) clothing that Fashion goes global, it is also through the 'intelligible'. All semiology, whatever the particularity or triviality of its object, is the search for this general intelligibility (which is not, because of this, permanently removed from the history or society in which it operates).[14] Therefore semiological analysis, even when it remains methodologically immanent to its object via its acceptance of the pertinence principle, itself demands a sociological dimension; however, we cannot then attach it back on to classical sociologies of 'knowledge', because the *intelligible* is not only – or perhaps ever – directly part of the *intellectual*; but rather it has to be inserted into the *socio-logic*, or sociology of classifications which Durkheim was already thinking about; so semiology is research into where things are *placed*, and not into the things themselves.

Having accepted the principle of pertinence and having also selected the particular sort of pertinence, the next step was to decide on the corpus of materials on which it was going to be brought to bear.[15] At first, we wanted to analyse the semantics of real clothes that are worn and not those of Fashion clothing.[16] This project was attractive because, as we have just said, it allowed us to link up with an authentic sociology of Fashion by studying its rhythms of renewal and its circuits of dissemination. But without even having to make a choice between a sociology of practices and a socio-logics of the intelligible, it was still difficult to undertake an initial 'exercise' in semiological analysis on an object that was probably full of meaning (real clothing is undeniably meaningful: humans communicate via clothes, tell each other if they are getting married, being buried, going hunting or to the beach, if they are department store staff or intellectuals, if they are doing their military service or painting), but in which finalities other than those of meaning remained extremely active (protection, ornamentation, economics), and which mixed, in a way which was tricky to discern, the individual act and the social institution, or what is termed, in Saussurian language, *parole* and *langue*. Since the object of the research was essentially the testing out of a method and not directly the discovery of a sociological truth, it was probably better to accept a simplification in all its openness, and to reduce the corpus by restricting it to descriptions of a particular clothing type, the sort covered in fashion publications and which we will call here fashion clothing.

But as well, although we still wanted to make sure that we remained in contact with the future tasks of a sociological study of real clothing, we restricted our analysis here to Fashion clothing, constituting a privileged object of semiological analysis as it does for three reasons. First, because those extra-semantic ends, which were, as we saw, such a nuisance to real clothing, are absent here: fashion clothing neither serves to protect nor to adorn but at best to signify protection by adornment: its being is entirely absorbed in its meaning. Second, since it is not being worn but only being *proposed*, Fashion clothing is a pure institution, devoid of all practical use; it is a *langue* without *parole*[17] and moreover this *langue* is artificial, elaborated not by the sum of users who are more or less conscious of their actions but by a group of decision-makers (the *fashion group*): Fashion clothing is, if you like, a logo-technics. Finally, Fashion clothing offers to the semiologist something human languages have always refused to the linguist: a pure synchrony; Fashion's synchrony changes suddenly every year but during that year it is absolutely stable: it is possible therefore to work on the fashionable without having to divide it up artificially as the linguist is obliged to do with the muddle of messages in a diachrony.[18]

Since it was a question of establishing the semantic system of fashion clothing in its institutional purity – and not its usage – the corpus was to be formed from that material which showed the clothing style with its origins, that is at the moment when it was artificially constituted in language and before being disseminated via real clothing; and it is this material that is found obviously in the fashion magazine. One might conceivably suggest that the small-scale models used by the big fashion designers, such as those sent to the studio or presentational models, constitute a purer corpus since they are closer to the logo-technical act; but precisely, this act is never fully finished until it reaches the fashion magazine stage, because it is the language of the magazine which gives the clothing created by haute couture the structure of a signifier and the power to signify; before being taken up by the fashion magazine, haute couture clothing (whether a small-scale model or a clothing range) is much closer to a working model than to a semantic unit (it is the prototype of a magical display, determining an act of fabrication, and its value is technological). Clothing that is meaningful in its entirety is to be found in the Fashion magazine (all the more so since the 'readership' here is massive), and therefore it is Fashion magazines which must constitute the corpus for our analysis.

Is this *all* Fashion magazines? Certainly not. Two types of limit on choices could be applied here, both authorised, and even recommended, by the stated aim of the research, which is to establish a formal system and not to describe a concrete Fashion, to provide the general 'grammar' of Fashion and not its sociology. First, those selected in relation to time; if we are looking for a structure, it is a good idea to work on only one state of Fashion, that is a synchronic one. Now, as we have said, the synchrony of Fashion is decided by fashion itself: it is the Fashion for one year.[19] For this we decided to work on the magazines from the year 1958–1959 (June to June), but this date obviously has no methodological importance; we could have chosen any other year, for what we were looking to describe was not such and such a Fashion, but *Fashion*; once collected, isolated from its year, the object (or utterance [*l'énoncé*]) found its place in a purely formal system of functions.[20] So there will be no indication here of any contingent Fashion, even less of a history of Fashion: we did not want to look at the substance of Fashion, but only at the structure of its signs.

Similarly (and here is the second limit placed on the corpus), there would have been no interest in going through all the magazines for one year unless we had wanted to isolate the substantial differences (ideological, aesthetic or social) between them; from a sociological point of view this would be a crucial issue, because each magazine would refer both to a socially defined audience and to a particular body of representations (and we have suggested continually how semantic analysis could help with this problem), but the differential sociology of magazines, audiences and ideologies was not the stated aim of this research: we have never aimed here at anything but a *pre-sociology* of Fashion.[21] So we went through in an exhaustive way only two magazines (*Elle* and *Jardin des Modes*), without denying the possibility of finding some things in other publications (mainly *Vogue* and *Echo de la Mode*[22]), as well as the weekly pages which certain daily newspapers provide on Fashion. What *was* important, given the semiological project, was to constitute a corpus which was reasonably saturated with all the possible *differences* in vestimentary signs; conversely, it did not matter if there was an element of repetition in these differences, for what makes meaning is not repetition but difference; structurally, a rare Fashion trait is as important as a frequent one, a gardenia as important as a long skirt; the aim here was to *distinguish* the units, not to count them.[23]

Having then established these principles, we needed to decide what we were looking for. The rule was obviously to work on the pure and homogenous units. So all the notations which could imply any finality other than meaning were removed from the inventory: such things as sales advertising, even if they seemed to describe a Fashion and the technical instructions for manufacture of the clothing (patterns). Neither did we retain make-up or hairstyle because, if these elements do indeed compete in terms of Fashion, they are nevertheless not made of the same material as clothing. There was still one formidable ambiguity: the occasions where photographed (or drawn) clothing and then clothing commented upon in a written text were mixed in the same magazine and often on the same page. These two systems obviously do not have the same substance; in one, it is looks, forms, surfaces, colours which count; in the other, sentences and words; so we had to sacrifice one of the two structures because in keeping both we could not hope to obtain homogenous units; we decided to opt for the system of verbalized clothing because in this system the verbal utterance of the Fashion signifieds constitutes an irreplaceable methodological advantage. So no Fashion photography will be treated,[24] and it is only the system of *written* Fashion clothing, provided by articulated language, that is reconstituted here.[25]

There are two ways of judging a piece of work: according to the project itself or according to how the project has been carried out. If we still have faith in the semiological project, we have nothing but doubts (and often unpleasant certainties) about how well it has been fulfilled here. It is not the dryness of this work, its abstraction, lack of 'ideas', its apparent distance from the big 'problems' of the world, it is not even the intuitive nature of certain purely empirical assertions which should have only been made with a commutative analysis, for which this work may be reproached.[26] On the contrary, it is its timidity in the face of formalism and its impotence in the face of the system; for, on the one hand, we were not able to avoid a certain number of subtle detours around substantialism, for example often giving a crypto-psychological description to the variants,[27] such is the inveterate naturalism in us; but against this, we did not know how, at many moments, to 'establish' elegantly (in the mathematical sense of the term) the system (or even how to tie it up or put it together),[28] leaving behind both 'holes' and assemblages which are perhaps useless;[29] some important theoretical points (for example the binary nature of oppositions) have not been cleared up; the belief upon which this work sits, that language is not the real, has perhaps led to a nominalism which was never defensible. So there would be fears that this series of failures might compromise the semiological project itself in the eyes of those who come into contact with this work, if we did not think that in the social sciences there was no definitive method (because the notion of *result* is itself illusory, evanescent) and that the capacity of a system to go wrong is as important as its capacity to work: therefore semiology will happily defer to a *new* system;[30] all it needs is for the latter to be able to take shape within the former – albeit clumsily.

## Notes

1. Published in *[VWA]* 25 (spring), 1998 [1963?], 'Le Cabinet des manuscrits', 7–28.

2. The word *Fashion* will be written with a capital to distinguish (clothing) Fashion from fashion in general (in the sense of vogue, or obsession: *fad* not *fashion*).

3. System: a collection of elements coordinated between each other. (Littré [dictionary].)

4. Lacan, and his reticence to Σ. See Jean Laplanche and Serge Leclaire [Editors' note: presumably this is a reference to Lacan's suspicion of assigning a signified, as discussed in Laplanche/Leclaire's 'L'inconscient' in *Les Temps Modernes* 183, July 1961, 81–129, see also Barthes's *Elements of Semiology*, 49].

5. Post-face to *Mythologies* [Editors' note: presumably Barthes is thinking of his reservations concerning semiological analysis as set out in 'Myth Today'].

6. 'Any description is acceptable on condition that it be coherent, that is to say that it be made from a *determinate point of view*. Once the viewpoint has been adopted, certain traits, known as pertinent, are to be isolated; the others, not pertinent, have to be discarded', André Martinet, *Eléments de linguistique générale*, Paris, Armand Colin, 1960, p. 38 [trans. Elizabeth Palmer, *Elements of General Linguistics*, London, Faber and Faber, 1964, p. 40; see also *Elements of Semiology*, 95, translated as 'principle of relevance'].

7. For the moment we hold to the normal meaning of the term; for a more precise meaning, in opposition to the semiological, cf. infra.

8. The idea that clothing signifies can be only a working hypothesis for the moment which will be justified later, cf. infra chapter 2. [Editors' note: Barthes is referring here to a putative chapter 2 of *The Fashion System*; however this debate over whether clothing signifies or not does not appear in the final book version.]

9. Fashion was from a very early stage (following Herbert Spencer) a central sociological object; firstly, it was 'a collective phenomenon, a typical mass phenomenon' (Stoetzel, *La Psychologie sociale*, Paris, Flammarion, 1963, 245). Secondly, it presented a dialectic of conformity and change which is explicable only sociologically; finally, its dissemination seems to depend upon those relay systems (with opinion leaders [Lazarsfeld's term] in between) which the sociologists Paul Lazarsfeld and Elihu Katz have studied [see *Personal Influence. The Part Played by People in the Flow of Mass Communications*, Report of Bureau of Applied Social Research, Columbia University, NY, Free Press, 1964, especially chapter XI 'Fashion Leaders', 247-270; see also *The Fashion System*, 9 n. 19] (Decatur [in the state of Illinois where Katz and Lazarsfeld carried out their research for *Personal Influence*], see also Lazarsfeld and

Raymond Boudon, *Le Vocabulaire des sciences sociales*, Paris/Hague, Mouton, 1965; and Paul Lazarsfeld, Hazel Gaudet, Bernard Berelson, *The People's Choice*, New York, Columbia University Press, 1948).

10. [See the work of Gilles-Gaston] Granger.

11. To this criterion certain authors add in a supplementary requirement, a double articulation (Georges Mounin ['Les analyses sémantiques', in *Cahiers de l'Institut de science économique appliquée*, March 1962, no. 123 (série M, no. 13), 105–124, where Mounin's main point is to stress that, though semantic analysis has been wisely applied to other disciplines such as sociology, anthropology, archaeology and psychology, it needs to be defined more carefully; in this vein, Mounin applauds the use of semantics in Barthes's *Mythologies* as a sociological and analytical tool, but he then regrets that 'sign', 'semantics' and 'semiology' are used by Barthes in the final essay 'Myth, Today' in their linguistic sense, only then to be 'confused', says Mounin, with the idea of 'symbol' as it is used in logic, psychology and psychoanalysis; this confusion, suggests Mounin, inhibits the interdisciplinary approach that Barthes tries to take in explaining myth (see p. 108 n. 6); see also *the Fashion System* 13.7 (197, on 'primitives' in language)] and André Martinet) [see *Elements of Semiology* 39, for Barthes's definition of double articulation].

12. [See the definition of clothing as language in] Hegel, Balzac, Michelet, Poe, Baudelaire, Proust.

13. 'Structural linguistics does not do away with non-linguistic languages… It is through the study of non-linguistic languages and by a comparison of these with linguistic languages that we will discover the *differentia specifica* of linguistic language.' (Louis Hjelmslev, *Essais linguistiques*, Copenhagen, Nordisk Sprog og Kulturforlag, 1959, in the Copenhagen Linguistic Circle series vol. 12, no. 14, p. 25).

14. Beliefs and ideologies point to the intelligible in which they participate, not through what they declare (their explicit content), but through the *manner in which* they declare it (their forms).

15. *Corpus*: intangible synchronic collection of utterances on which one is working (Martinet, *Eléments*, p. 37 [English trans. p. 39]; see note 6).

16. Barthes, 'Language and Clothing' [see chapter 2 in this book].

17. On this problem, see infra.

18. The notion of language synchrony is one of the most disputed in structural linguistics – reservations made by Paul Guillaume [see his *La Psychologie de la forme*, Paris, Flammarion, 1979 (first published in 1930), esp. 200–04, and chapter VIII], R. Jakobson, and Cl. Lévi-Strauss, *Anthropologie structurale*, p. 102 [trans. by Claire Jacobson and Brooke Grundfest Schoepf, NY/London, Basic Books, 1963, 88–89; this is Lévi-Strauss's critique of Haudricourt and Granai's 1955 collaborative work on 'linguistics and sociology', in which Lévi-Strauss uses Jakobson to show that synchrony and diachrony are separate only in a theoretical sense].

19. There are seasonal Fashions within any one year; but the seasons are not so much a diachronic series as a selection of different signifieds; in its 'essence' Fashion changes but once a year (this is the 'look').

20. We are even not worried that we used examples from other synchronies when we needed to check something or when there was an interesting example.

21. In fact this differential sociology remains problematic; for mass society develops perhaps collective representations which from then on become universal: the *socius* goes back to being the *anthros*.

22. This choice was not however arbitrary: *Elle* and *Echo de la Mode* are popular magazines (the latter more so than the former), and *Vogue* and *Jardin des Modes* more 'aristocratic'.

23. Disparity in frequency is important for sociology, but not for a system; it tells us something about the tastes, the 'obsessions' of a particular magazine (and therefore of its audience), but not about the general structure.

24. We have therefore adopted a restricted definition of Fashion in relation to that given by Lazarsfeld and Katz (aesthetics, make-up, clothes).

25. The Fashion utterances [*les énoncés*] are cited without references: for, in the semiological inventory, they have a purely functional and not historical value, following exactly the examples of grammarians.

26. For example, how to structure the variant in Form or how to list typical associations. But these empirical or intuitive notations have been accepted to the extent that they allowed us to move (in the final stages) towards an inventory of real clothing (notably the infringements upon the rules of terminology) and more generally intuition seemed difficult to disassociate from a research project in its infancy.

27. The variants of continuity for example could be defined only through their layout in the grid; so a clothing item, like the part of the body where it is worn, is not linked to the mobility variant (syntagmatic definition).

28. Notably for the assertion of types.

29. Perhaps we could be more economical with the *object in hand*, that is with the ternary matrix, by developing the system towards two-term routines.

30. What increases the chances of defects in the $\Sigma$ [signified] is that it is a classificatory activity; and classifying is (subjectively) an act of intense but rapid (even voracious) assimilation; in all classification there is an element of perhaps premature destruction of the object.

# 8

# *Fashion, a Strategy of Desire*

## *Round-table Discussion with Roland Barthes, Jean Duvignaud and Henri Lefebvre*[1]

*Fashion is changing. Short skirts, loud colours, boys in long shirts and girls in trousers. Women's liberation? Loss of male virility? It is not so simple. So we asked three sociologists to consider this debate, apparently frivolous but which they are studying very seriously. Henri Lefebvre, Professor at the Sorbonne, is amongst other things the author of* A Sociology of Everyday Life; *he is currently working on a study* Fashion and Culture.[2] *Professor at the Ecole des Hautes Etudes, Roland Barthes is, as we know, the author of* Mythologies *and has for a long time been teaching a course on 'the Fashion System' using women's magazines. As for Jean Duvignaud, Professor at the University of Orleans, his recent books on theatre (*Sociology of Theatre, *and* The Actor) *incline him to see in fashion an extension of theatrical performance.*

**Le Nouvel Observateur:** *How is the sociologist interested by fashion?*

**Roland Barthes:** Fashion has been a privileged object for sociologists since Spencer. Fashion is a phenomenon both of innovation and conformity. So there is a paradox here which cannot but hold the attention of sociologists. We all follow fashion and, in theory, it is made up only of what is new. There is then a sort of contradiction in terms. You have to imitate that which is in fashion in order not to be imitable...

*Henri Lefebvre:* Yes, just so long as we do not restrict fashion to clothing. Fashion is also concerned as much with literature, painting, music... It is a general phenomenon. The study of fashion can be particularized by looking at clothing but it is the whole of society which is implicated.

*Jean Duvignaud:* To stick with clothing fashion, I get the impression that, since the revolution brought about by Paul Poiret – getting rid of the corset, shortening of skirts etc. – fashion has been a way for women of displaying their existence, in a society dominated by masculine values. Notice how women's fashion is, by and large, defined and thought about by men.

*HL:* It plays with the material or visual forms proposed by men; but, so as these are absorbed by women, there must be something however which originates with women...

*RB:* A pseudo-psychoanalyst in America says that men often create aberrant forms of fashion to avenge themselves on women, to disfigure them.[3]

*JD:* When fashion undresses women in the way that today's does, it is not to disfigure them... Since the 1920s we have seen an explosion in new forms, in the varieties of forms to be combined, which suggests a much greater freedom.

*Le NO: In your view, does a woman dress for herself rather than, for example, to please men?*

*HL:* Here we are in a very ambiguous domain, linked to the 'hygiene' of clothes, which is there both to veil and to show what it is hiding, to dissimulate or to suggest something other than what it is revealing. The trick is the way in which this ambiguity is used.

*RB:* It is for this reason that, psychoanalytically, clothing has been likened to a neurosis, a slight neurosis, to the precise extent that it hides and advertises at the same time. In his *Psychology of Clothes*, the Englishman Flügel provides a psychological interpretation for the increase in the number of clothes. He cites the example of oriental peoples, for whom wearing a dress is a sign of authority. In modern Western civilization, the super-Ego is manifested in the tight collar, etc. But here, we are getting away from fashion.

*Le NO: And above all from these new fashions, from short skirts, for example, which embarrass so many men...*

*HL:* When men and women meet there is a perpetual tension. The women never stop striking up poses, changing their body line, adjusting their skirt to the right length, or, on the contrary, revealing themselves. The men no longer know what they can and should look at... This malaise is at the same time useful for communication – or at least it does not interrupt it. You might say that designers maintain this tension on purpose...

*JD:* In the regions of the world where women go around naked, the arrival of clothing made of printed material made the women more desired by the men. It is almost like Baudelaire's idea of the *femme parée:* nudity is attractive only when culture recreates it.[4]

*HL:* In the case of fashion, it is merely a question of a superficial eroticization of human relationships which are not resolved by this.

*RB:* The great historical prototypes of fashion only change every fifty years. The oscillations are very regular and historical events do not affect them. Of course, within these rhythms, there are micro-variations: skirt length, for example, can change several times in ten years. But the global rhythm is not affected by these micro-variations. After a period of short skirts, we will automatically have a period of long skirts.

*HL:* Today, class phenomena are becoming blurred or are disappearing. But for a long time it was the women of the bourgeoisie who would wear long skirts, whereas lower-class women wore short skirts... But contrary to what Barthes was saying, I think that technical developments do influence fashion. Around 1920 we had the petite aviatrix, now we have the petite cosmonaut.

*RB:* I always resist linking historical content to clothing forms.

*JD:* There are perhaps no direct links between fashion and history, but there are links with certain key changes within societies.

*Le NO: Many women think that today's fashion is not 'comfortable'. Daily life, the car, would suggest other forms of clothing for them.*

*RB:* In reality fashion is never functional, never utilitarian. If women bought dresses only when they needed them, if a society bought clothes only because of wear and tear, there wouldn't be any fashion: the buying rhythm must be faster than that of clothing wearing out.

*HL:* What bothers me in what you are saying is that you allow no space for invention. There are nevertheless technologies, forms, new materials…

*RB:* An invention which is purely that of combining remains an invention. A limited number of elements to be combined can produce the impression, a justified one, of a creation.

*JD:* It used to be the case that the manifestations of women's fashion were the forms of theatrical representation reserved for an elite. Nowadays, the acting takes place in the street. Never have aspirations towards performance been as pronounced as today. With its aspects of fantasy, fashion corresponds to a need for a theatricalization in our lives as they become less and less authentic. We are going towards an affirmation of individual existence but one which is destroyed by industrial society, towards the need to create a false existence which we then want to become true.

*Le NO: Fashion today lays emphasis also on youth.*

*RB:* More than youth, we should speak of a 'junior style', as defined by the boutiques on *Rue de la Pompe,*[5] with elements borrowed from the fleamarket: a junior fashion where the two sexes take on values which are hard to distinguish.

*JD:* Here we are seeing the need to exist through costume…

*HL:* What is rather strange, since fashion is mimetic, is the way people claim a personality via a model.

*RB:* We have not talked enough about the profoundly narcissistic and erotic value of clothes. That includes all fashions. However, paradoxically, I would say that there is not any 'figure' of fashion which is erotic in itself; a body which is completely covered can be deemed as erotic by society. Eroticism is linked to the contrast in norms in any one society; taking off clothes is not an erotic act in itself.

*HL: Strategy of Desire* is the title of a book on advertising…

*RB:* Yes, by Dichter, an American 'psychoanalyst', consulted all over the world by advertisers of cigars, beer, fashion etc. He is absolutely right about what is going to be fashionable over the next few years.

*Le NO: Well, what is it going to be?*

**RB:** We will see, in clothes, the further attenuation of the difference between the sexes. Men will wear perfume. Women will have tattoos...[6]

*HL:* Let's not forget that fashion is a game. Getting dressed up is wanting to play.

## Notes

1. Published in *Le Nouvel-Observateur* 71 (23 March 1966), 28–29, in the 'Women's condition' column.

2. [Editors' note: no doubt an early title for Lefebvre's *La Vie quotidienne dans le monde moderne*, first published in 1968; Lefebvre had earlier published a *Critique de la vie quotidienne* in 1947 (republished in 1958), and then a second volume, *Fondements d'une sociologie de la quotidienneté*, in 1962.]

3. [Editors' note: Barthes is almost certainly referring to Edmund Bergler M. D., *Fashion and the Unconscious*, New York, Robert Brunner, 1953.]

4. [Editors' note: Duvignaud is referring to Baudelaire's idea that women's bodies and the clothes that cover them are 'an indivisible totality'. See *Le Peintre de la vie moderne*, in Charles Baudelaire, *Curiosités esthétiques*, Paris, Garnier Frères, 1962, 486–490 (translated as *The Painter of Modern Life and Other Essays*, by Jonathan Mayne, New York, Da Capo Press, 1985).]

5. [Editors' note: smart and chic street of clothing boutiques in the bourgeois sixteenth arrondissement of Paris.]

6. [Editors' note: see E. Dichter, *Strategy of Desire*, London, T. V. Boardman & Co., 1960, 244.]

# 9

# *Fashion and the Social Sciences*[1]

Fashion consists of imitating that which has first shown itself as inimitable. This mechanism, paradoxical at first glance, is all the more interesting to sociology in that this discipline is principally concerned with modern, technical, industrial societies and fashion is a phenomenon which historically is particular to these societies. It must be pointed out that there are peoples and societies without fashion, for example ancient Chinese society, where clothing was strictly coded in an almost immutable way. The absence of fashion corresponded to the totally stagnant nature of society.

For civilizations without writing, fashion poses a very interesting problem, though this has hardly been studied. This problem belongs to the sociology of cultural exchange: in countries like those in the new Africa, traditional, indigenous clothing, clothing that is unchanging and not subject to fashion, comes up against the phenomenon of fashion originating in the West. This results in compromises, especially for women's clothing. The major 'patterns', models and forms of indigenous clothing are often maintained either in the shape and the form of the clothing or in the types of colours and designs employed; but the clothing is subject to the fashion rhythms of the West, that is to an annual production of fashion and to a renewal of detail. What is interesting in this occurrence is the meeting of a vestimentary civilization not based on fashion with the phenomenon of fashion. It seems that we could conclude that fashion is not linked to such and such a particular form of clothing but rather is exclusively a question of rhythm, a question of rate in time.

Fashion poses a more acute and more paradoxical problematic to historians than it does to sociologists. The sort of public opinion maintained and promoted by the press and its letters pages etc. presents fashion as an essentially capricious phenomenon, based on the creative faculty of the designer. According to public opinion, fashion is still located within a mythology of unfettered creativity that enables it to evade both the systematic and the habitual, resting upon a rather romantic notion of an inexhaustible abundance of spontaneous creativity. Isn't it said that fashion designers can do anything with nothing?

Historians, or to be more accurate, ethnologists have studied this creative aspect of fashion. The well-known American ethnologist Kroeber made a rich and in-depth study of women's evening dress in the West, stretching back about three centuries and using reproductions of engravings. Having adjusted the dimensions of these plates due to their diverse origins, he was able to analyse the constant elements in fashion features and to come up with a study that was neither intuitive nor approximate, but precise, mathematical and statistical. He reduced women's clothing to a certain number of features: length and size of the skirt, size and depth of the neckline, height of the waistline.[2] He demonstrated unambiguously that fashion is a profoundly regular phenomenon which is not located at the level of annual variations but on the scale of history. For practically 300 years, women's dress was subject to a very precise periodic oscillation: forms reach the furthest point in their variations every fifty years. If, at any one moment, skirts are at their longest, fifty years later they will be at their shortest; thus skirts become long again fifty years after being short and a hundred years after being long.

Kroeber also showed regular connections between, for example, the variations in the length of the skirt and the width of the neckline; certain features are linked in the rhythm of fashion.

The historian is presented here with a fascinating problem, namely that of a particular cultural system which appears to escape all historical determinants. So the West has seen, in 300 years, many changes of regime, many evolutions and many ideological, sentimental and religious upheavals; and yet none of these important historical events has had any effect on the content or even on the rhythms of fashion. The French Revolution did not really fundamentally change this rhythm. No one in their right mind can establish the slightest link between a high waistline and the Consulate; the most one can say is that major historical events can speed up or slow down the absolutely regular returns of certain fashions.

Men's clothing has a slightly different history from that of women's clothing. Contemporary Western men's clothing was constituted in its general form (*basic pattern*) at the start of the nineteenth century and was influenced by two factors. The first is a formal factor coming from England: men's clothing originates in the Quaker outfit (tight, buttoned jacket, in neutral colours). The second factor is an ideological one. The democratization of society led to the promotion of the values of work over idleness, and developed in men an ideology of self-respect, originating with the English. In the Anglomania at the end of the eighteenth century, self-control found itself incarnated in France in the archetypically austere, constrained and closed nature of male clothing. This clothing ensured that class differences were not visible.

Prior to this, societies had clothing which was completely coded, with any difference depending on whether one belonged to the aristocracy, to the bourgeoisie or to the world of the peasant. As part of the democratization process, the many types of male apparel disappeared, leaving one type of clothing. But just as the suppression of social classes at the start of the nineteenth century was illusory (for these classes continued to exist), so men belonging to the upper classes were obliged, so as to distinguish themselves from the masses, to vary the detail on their outfits, since they were no longer able to change their form. They elaborated this new notion, which was not at all democratic, and called it *distinction* – the word is suitably ambiguous. It was a question of distinguishing oneself in social terms; by distinguishing oneself socially, one was, one is, 'distinguished'. From this we get dandyism: the extremely refined choice of details. A man in the nineteenth century, no longer able to modify the form of his jacket, would distinguish himself from the common man by the manner in which he tied his cravat or wore his gloves...

Since then men's clothing has not really undergone any major changes. But today, a new phenomenon can be seen evolving:

the growth of a truly young person's clothing. Up until now, the young person, even the child, did not wear any outfits specific to them: children were dressed like adults, but using smaller models. Then we saw the appearance of clothing for children, followed by a fashion for young people. This latter is becoming an imperative, imperialist even; to the extent that we must now study men's fashion in terms of adolescent fashion.

In this domain there are micro-sociological phenomena, micro-fashions; these change about every two years. There used to be blue jeans, black jacket, leather jacket; now we have the *Rockers* fashion: tight jacket like that worn by Alfred de Musset, very long hair... This masculine fashion can be found only in young people, juniors.

Clothing – I am not talking about fashion – knows three timescales, three rhythms, three histories.

One of the discoveries of contemporary historical science has been to show that historical time cannot be conceived of as linear and unique because history is made up of a number of timescales of different lengths which lie over each other. There are absolutely specific events; there are *situations* of longer duration called *conjunctures*; and finally there are *structures* which last even longer.

Clothing is affected by all three of these timescales. The longest covers the archetypal forms of clothing in a given civilization. For centuries and within a specific geographical area, oriental men wore, and still wear in part, a dress; in Japan it is the kimono, in Mexico the poncho, etc. This is the *basic pattern*, the basic model for a civilization. Within this timescale moderate but perfectly regular variations take place.[3] The third timescale in short could be called the time of micro-fashions. We can see this in our Western civilization today when fashion changes every year. In fact, these annual variations interest the press and commerce more than they actually affect the general model. We are subjected to a kind of optical illusion which makes us attribute great importance to the annual variation in forms whereas in fact, in historical terms, these variations are merely part of larger, regular rhythms.

There may be a problem one day if the perfectly regular half-century rhythm of fashion were to change. A dress would then normally reach its shortest length in ten or twenty years, then pass through the apparent return of the long dress, and then the cycle would start again with the long dress passing through the apparent return of the short one. We might think that, if this rhythm were shaken up, skirts would probably remain short. It would be interesting to study this phenomenon and link a shake-up of the rhythm to something happening in the history of contemporary civilization...

If Kroeber's rhythm were disrupted, it might be due to the growth and globalization of culture, of clothing, of food and by a kind of equalization of cultural objects, of a jostling together that is so intense that the fashion rhythm would be changed. A new history of fashion will begin.

Changes in rhythm belong to no one. The expression 'a fashion has come from America' is very ambiguous as it is true and false at the same time. Change, supposedly brought about by a fashion, has no origin: it is in the formal law which governs the human mind and in the rotations of these forms in the world. However the origins of the content of fashion can indeed be located, that is the borrowing of a form or a detail which exist already, such as the hairstyle of an actor or an actress, or the way of wearing a dress. Emerging from this question of origins is the notion of mastering fashion, but this very complicated subject is secondary and does not directly interest sociology.

Some people want sociologists to say that the men's fashion for long hair comes from the Beatles; this is correct, but it would be wrong to construct the personality of today's young man in this way and to induce that there is a feminization, or a laziness, of character taking place because of long hair. If hair has become long, it is because it was short before. I am summarizing (and in a rather brusque fashion) my ideas here because I subscribe to a formalist interpretation of the fashion phenomenon. It seems a bit misleading to stuff a phenomenon full of apparently natural contents, none of which are anything of the sort. People who write on the subject of clothing are always tempted to make these psychological links. To consider variations as part of a feminization of clothing seems illusory to me. There is no feature of clothing which is naturally feminine; all there is is a rotation, regular turn-arounds of forms.

What is at stake in clothing is a particular meaning of the body, of the person. Hegel was already saying that clothes made the body meaningful and that therefore they allowed the move to be made from simple feeling to meaning. Psychoanalysts too have concerned themselves with the meaning of clothes. Flügel, using Freudian categories, has analysed clothing,[4] and shown that dressing functioned for Man as a kind of neurosis; since it simultaneously both hides and advertises the body in exactly the same way that neurosis hides and reveals what a person does not want to say by exhibiting symptoms and symbols. Clothing would in some way be analogous to the phenomenon that reveals our feelings when we blush; our face turns red, we hide our embarrassment at the very moment when we are advertising it.

Clothing concerns all of the human person, all the body, all the relationships of Man to body as well as the relationships of the body to society, which explains why great writers have often been preoccupied by dressing in their works. We can find beautiful pages on this subject in Balzac, Baudelaire, Edgar Poe, Michelet, Proust; they all realized that clothing was an element which involved, as it were, the whole of being.

Sartre treats this question from a philosophical point of view when he shows that clothing allows Man to 'assume his freedom', to constitute himself as he chooses, even if what he has chosen to be represents what others have chosen for him: society made Genet into a thief, and so Genet chooses to be a thief. Clothing is very close to this phenomenon; it seems that it has interested writers and philosophers because of its links with personality, of its capacity to change one's being for another; personality makes fashion; it makes clothing; but inversely, clothing makes personality. There is certainly a dialectic between these two elements. The final answer depends on our own personal philosophy.

In the eighteenth century many books were written on clothing. They were descriptive works but were based explicitly, and very consciously, on the *coding* of clothes, that is on the link between certain types of dressing with certain professions, with certain social classes, certain towns and certain regions. Clothing was perceived as a kind of language, as a kind of grammar: the clothes code. So we can see that clothing is part of that very busy activity in which every object is given a meaning. For all time, clothing has been the object of codification.

This brings us to revise a traditional point of view that at first glance seems reasonable and which maintained that Man invented clothing for three reasons: as protection against harsh weather, out of modesty for hiding nudity and for ornamentation to get noticed. This is all true. But we must add another function, which seems to me to be more important: the function of meaning. Man has dressed himself in order to carry out a signifying activity. The wearing of an item of clothing is fundamentally an act of meaning that goes beyond modesty, ornamentation and protection. It is an act of signification and therefore a profoundly social act right at the very heart of the dialectic of society.

## Notes

1. Interview published in *Echanges*, Assumption 1966; *Oeuvres complètes* vol. 2, 121–25.

2. Kroeber and Richardson, *Three Centuries of Women's Fashion*, Berkeley, University of California Press, 1940.

3. Those variations observed by Kroeber and Richardson.

4. Flügel, *Psychology of Clothes*, London, Hogarth, 1950.

# 10

# *On* The Fashion System[1]

*F. Gaussen: The Fashion System presents itself as a 'book on method' with reference to semiology. Could you tell us what semiology is?*

*Roland Barthes:* It was Saussure who first postulated the existence of a general science of signs, which he had called semiology. He thought that linguistics would be only a part of this science. This semiological project was then taken up thanks to the development of linguistics and of the social sciences. People came to the conclusion that many cultural objects used by humans constituted systems of communication and therefore of meaning. One could say that all of culture, in the widest sense of the word, is beholden to a science of meaning. The most seemingly utilitarian of objects – food, clothes, shelter – and especially those which are based on language such as literature (whether good or bad literature), press stories, advertising etc., invite semiological analysis.

*FG: Is it possible to distinguish signs that are totally independent of language?*

*RB:* Obviously we could mention very elementary systems such as the highway code or aircraft landing signs. But, in my view, I'm certain that the study of non-linguistic signs is an abstraction, a utopia. Real culture contains only objects which are full of human language, whether it be in description, commentary, or conversation... Our civilization is a civilization of the written word as much as it is one of the image. Written language has very precise functions of abstraction, of knowledge, of choice of meanings. To live in a civilization purely of the image would create a certain anxiety because the image always has several meanings. It is for this reason that photos in newspapers are always captioned: to reduce the risk engendered by a multiplicity of meanings.

*FG: Your study seems to rest on a certain paradox. That is, though fashion deploys very varied systems of expression, especially the image, you have chosen to limit your research to the written description of clothes, as found in magazines such as* Elle *or* Jardin des Modes. *Why?*

*RB:* Originally I had planned to study real clothing, worn by everyone in the street. I gave up. The reason for this is that fashion clothing is complex in that it deploys a number of 'substances': the material, photography, language... Now, there has not been any applied semiological work carried out as yet. It was necessary to give priority to problems of method. Because of this I preferred to choose an object as 'pure' as possible to analyse, that is one which rests on a single 'substance'. I studied fashion clothing as it is refracted through the written language of specialist magazines. All I retained was the description, that is the transformation of an object into language.

Originally this work was meant to be in some way the start of a general programme of semiology which would have covered all the cultural systems in our civilization: clothes, food, the city... But, inspired by new research, this semiological project itself is evolving and it is starting to encounter the specific problems generated by the objects it is trying to analyse: are we right to constitute food for example as a system of signs? However limited this book on fashion may be, it poses the problem of knowing if there really is an object that we call fashion clothing.

*FG: This 'Fashion System' breaks down into two systems.*

*RB:* Indeed. It is all about detecting in one simple message – the description of a fashionable dress – the overlaying of a number of systems of meaning: on the one hand, what we might call the 'vestimentary code' which controls a certain number of different usages, and on the other the rhetoric, that is the way in which the magazine expresses this code and which itself reflects a certain vision of the world, an ideology. Semiological analysis allows us to situate the place of ideology within the general system of meanings, without, of course, being able to go any further, since the description of particular ideologies belongs to another science.

*FG: What guarantee of objectivity does the semiologist have in the analysis he makes of this rhetoric?*

**RB:** Obviously the analysis of rhetoric requires the researcher to rely on their own feeling as a reader, something which might shock the positivist procedures associated with experimentation. As soon as we study language, we come up against this obstacle. There is no 'proof' of language other than its readability, its immediate understanding. In order to prove the analysis of a language being made you have always to come back to the 'linguistic sentiment' of the person who is speaking. In any case, my exteriority to the language that I am analysing is only provisional. Indeed, my own description itself could in turn be taken up by another wider and more coherent system of explanation. I think that semiology is an accurate method, but this accuracy can itself become the object of other languages. I do not have a positivist feeling with regard to semiology; rather a historical one.

*FG: Your study presents itself as a kind of syntax of semiology. It works hard to create units, rules, categories. Do you think that this method has a universal value and could be applied to any object?*

**RB:** This way of researching, which by the way is not original and comes from linguistics, may provisionally have a universal value as a method of discovery. It involves breaking things down into units, classifying them and examining their rules of combination, like a grammarian. Obviously, if the object changes, the method itself must be modified. Classifications will turn out differently.

*FG: What image of fashion have you kept from your analysis?*

**RB:** The title of my book, *The Fashion System*, is pure provocation. For me fashion is indeed a system. Contrary to the myth of improvisation, of caprice, of fantasy, of free creativity, we can see that fashion is strongly coded. It is ruled by combination in which there is a finite reserve of elements and certain rules of change. The whole set of fashion features for each year is found in the collection of features which has its own rules and limits, like grammar. These are purely formal rules. For example, there are some elements of clothing that can be put together, but others which are not allowed.

If fashion appears to us to be unpredictable this is because we are using only a small human memory. As soon as we widen it to its historical dimension we find a very marked regularity.

The second image of fashion that I have taken from my analysis is a more ethical one, more a part of my own preoccupations. It seemed to me that there were two fashions. On the one hand, fashion tries hard to make the written item of clothing correspond to uses, characters, seasons, functions: '*A dress for evening wear, for shopping, for spring, for the student, for the carefree young girl...*'. Here the arbitrary nature of fashion is sidestepped, hidden beneath this rationalized, naturalist lexicon. Fashion is lying. It is hiding behind social and psychological alibis.

On the other hand there is another vision of fashion which rejects this system of equivalences and sets up a truly abstract and poetic function. This is a fashion of idleness, of luxury, but which has the merit of declaring itself as pure form. In this way it becomes part of literature. A fascinating example of this literary connection is supplied by Mallarmé who wrote, just for himself, a little fashion magazine: *La Dernière Mode*. This was a real fashion magazine, with descriptions of dresses such as you might find, minus the talent, in *Elle*. But, at the same time, these descriptions are, for the author, a deeply important, almost metaphysical, exercise using the Mallarméan themes of nothingness, of the trinket, of inanity. It is an emptiness which is not absurd, a nothingness which is constructed as a meaning.

*FG: You indicate in your preface that your research is 'already dated'. What do you mean?*

*RB:* This study uses operational concepts – 'sign, signifier, signified' – which if not challenged have been at least considerably remodelled by research these past few years, by people such as Lévi-Strauss and Lacan. This vocabulary is being somewhat questioned at the moment. Thinking about meaning has become enriched but also divided, with antagonisms appearing. From this point of view, my research looks a little naive. It is an 'untamed' semiology. But I will say in my defence that these rather fixed concepts are in fact applied to an object which is a profound part of mass culture, part of a certain alienation. Mass society always tends to get stuck on defined, named, separated meanings. This is why the fixed concepts that I use are those which go the best with fashion. They may be simplistic in the way they describe what is going on in the depths of the human psyche, but they retain all their pertinence when it comes to analysing our society.

## *Note*

1. Interview with F. Gaussen, published in *Le Monde*, 19 April 1967; *Oeuvres complètes* vol. 2, 462–64.

# Part III

# Fashion Debates and Interpretations

# 11

# *The Contest between Chanel and Courrèges. Refereed by a Philosopher*[1]

If today you open a history of our literature, you should find there the name of a new classical author: Coco Chanel. Chanel does not write with paper and ink (except in her leisure time), but with material, with forms and with colours; however, this does not stop her being commonly attributed with the authority and the panache of a writer of the classical age: elegant like Racine, Jansenist like Pascal (whom she quotes), philosophical like La Rochefoucauld (whom she imitates by delivering her own maxims to the public), sensitive like Madame de Sévigné and, finally, rebellious like the 'Grande Mademoiselle' whose nickname and function she borrows (see for example her recent declarations of war on fashion designers).[2] Chanel, it is said, keeps fashion on the edge of barbarism all the more to overwhelm it with all the values of the classical order: reason, nature, permanence, the desire to charm and not to surprise; people are pleased to see Chanel in the pages of the *Figaro* newspaper where she occupies, alongside Cocteau, the fringes of polite culture.

What would be the extreme opposite of this classicism if not futurism? Courrèges, it is said, dresses women from the year 2000 who are already the young girls of today. Mixing, as in all legends, the person's character with the style of the works produced, Courrèges is credited with the mythical qualities of the absolute innovator: young, tempestuous, galvanic, virulent, mad on sport (and the most abrupt of these – rugby), keen on rhythm (the presentation of his outfits is accompanied by jerky music), rash to the point of being contradictory as he invents an evening dress which is not a dress (but a pair of shorts). Tradition, common sense and feeling – without which there is no good hero in France – are tightly controlled by him and only appear discreetly at the edges of his private life: he likes walking alongside his mountain stream at home, draws like an artist and sends the only black dress in his collection to his mother in Pau.

All this means that everyone feels that there is something important that separates Chanel and Courrèges – perhaps something more profound than fashion or at least something for which fashion is simply the means by which it presents itself. What might this be?

The creations by Chanel challenge the very idea of fashion. Fashion (as we conceive it today) rests on a violent sensation of time. Every year fashion destroys that which it has just been admiring, it adores that which it is about to destroy; last year's fashion, now destroyed, could offer to the victorious fashion of the current year an unfriendly word such as the dead leave to the living and which can be read on certain tombstones: *I was yesterday what you are today, you will be tomorrow what I am today*. Chanel's work does not take part at all – or only slightly – in this annual vendetta. Chanel always works on the same model which she merely 'varies' from year to year, as one might 'vary' a musical theme; her work says (and she herself confirms it) that there is an 'eternal' beauty of woman, whose unique image is relayed to us by art history; she rejects with indignation perishable materials, paper, plastic, which are sometimes used in America to make dresses. The very thing that negates fashion, long life, Chanel makes into a precious quality.

Now, in the aesthetics of clothing there is a very particular, even paradoxical, value which ties seduction to long life: that is 'chic'; 'chic' can handle and even demands if not the worn look, at least usage; 'chic' cannot stand the look of newness (we recall that the dandy Brummell would never wear an outfit without having aged it a little on the back of his servant). 'Chic', this sublimated time, is the key value in Chanel's style. Courrèges' ensembles by contrast do not have this fear: very fresh, colourful, even brightly coloured, the dominant colour in them is white, the absolute new; this deliberately extreme youthful fashion, with its school and sometimes childlike, even infantile, references (baby's shoes and socks), and for which even winter is a time for light colours, is continually brand new and does not suffer from any complexes as it dresses brand new beings. From Chanel to Courrèges the 'grammar' of timescales changes: the unchanging 'chic' of Chanel tells us that the woman has already lived (and has known how to); the obstinate 'brand-newness' of Courrèges that she is going to live.

So it is the notion of time, which is a *style* for one and a *fashion* for the other, that separates Chanel from Courrèges, as does a particular idea of the body. It is not a coincidence that Chanel's own invention, the woman's suit, is very close to men's clothing. The man's suit and the woman's suit by Chanel have one ideal in common: 'distinction'. In the nineteenth century 'distinction' was a social value; in a society which had recently been democratized and in which men from the upper classes were not now permitted to advertise their wealth – but which their wives were allowed to do for them by proxy – it allowed them to 'distinguish' themselves all the same by using a discreet detail. The Chanel style picks up on this historical heritage in a filtered, feminized way and it is this, furthermore, which paradoxically makes it very dated; the Chanel style corresponds to that rather brief moment in our history (which is part of Chanel's own youth) when a minority of women went out to work and had social independence and therefore it had to transpose into clothing something of men's values, beginning with this famous 'distinction', the only luxury option open to men now that work had standardized them. The Chanel woman is not the idle young girl but the young woman confronting the world of work which is itself kept discreet, evasive; of this world of work she allows to be read from her clothing, from her supple suit that is both practical and distinguished, not its content (it is not a uniform), but work's compensation, a higher form of leisure, cruises, yachts, sleeper carriages, in short modern, aristocratic travel, as celebrated by Paul Morand and Valery Larbaud. So, of all the fashions, the Chanel style is perhaps, paradoxically, the most social, because what it fights, what it rejects, are not, as one might think, the futurist provocations of the new fashion designs but rather the vulgarities of petty bourgeois clothing; so it is in societies confronted with a newly arisen need for aesthetic self-promotion, in Moscow – where she often goes – that Chanel has the best chance of being the most successful.

There is however a price to pay for the Chanel style: a certain forgetting of the body which we would say takes refuge, is absorbed, in the social 'distinction' of clothing. It is not Chanel's fault: from her earliest career something new has appeared in our society which the new fashion designers are trying to translate, to codify; a new social class, unforeseen by sociologists, has been born – youth. As the body is its only asset, youth does not need to be vulgar or 'distinguished': it simply *is*. Take the Chanel woman: we can locate her social milieu, her jobs, her leisure activities, her travels. Then take the Courrèges woman: we do not ask what she does, who her parents are, what her income is – she is young, necessarily and sufficiently so. Both simultaneously abstract and material, Courrèges fashion seems to have assigned itself only one function: that of making clothing into a very clear sign for the whole body. A sign does not necessarily involve exhibiting (fashion is always chastened); it is said, perhaps too often, that the short skirt 'shows' the leg. Such things are bit more complicated than that. What probably matters to a designer like Courrèges is not the very material stripping off that annoys everyone, but rather to provide women's clothing with that *allusive* expression which makes the body appear close, without ever exhibiting it, to bring us into a new relationship with the young bodies all around us, by suggesting to us, via a whole play of forms, colours and details that is the art of clothes designing, that we *could* strike up a friendship with these young people. The whole Courrèges style is contained in this conditional, for which the female body is the stake: it is the conditional tense that we find in jackets with very short sleeves (which show no nudity at all, but register in our minds the idea of audacity), it is in the florid transparency of evening-wear shorts, in the new two-piece dresses worn for dancing that are flimsy like underwear, in this fashion without attachments (in the real and figurative sense) in which the body always seems to be close, friendly and seductive, simple and decent.

So, on one side we have tradition (with its internal acts of re-newal), and on the other innovation (with its implicit constants); here classicism (albeit in sensitive mode), there modernism (albeit in mundane mode). We have to believe that society needs this contest, because society has been ingenious at launching it – at least for the last few centuries – in all domains of art, and in an infinite variety of forms; and if we now see it clearly breaking into fashion, it is because fashion too is also an art, in the same way as literature, painting and music are.

What is more, the Chanel-Courrèges contest teaches us – or rather confirms to us – the following: today, thanks to the formidable growth of the means of communication such as the press, television, the cinema even, fashion is not only what women wear, it is also what all women (and all men) look at and read about: our fashion designers' inventions please, or annoy us, just like a novel, a film or a record. We project on to Chanel suits for women and on to Courrèges shorts everything that is to do with beliefs, prejudices and resistances, in short the whole of one's own personal history, what we call in one (perhaps simplistic) word: taste.

And all this suggests perhaps a way of understanding the Chanel-Courrèges contest (if at least you have no intention of buying either Chanel or Courrèges). As part of this broad everyday culture in which we participate through everything we read and see, the Chanel style and Courrèges fashion set up an opposition which is much less a matter of choice than something to be interpreted. Chanel and Courrèges, these two names are like the two rhymes in the same couplet or the contrasting exploits of a couple of heroes without which there is no nice story. If we want to keep these two sides of the same sign together, and undifferentiated – that is, the sign of our times – then fashion will have been made into a truly poetic subject, constituted collectively, so that we are then presented with the profound spectacle of an ambiguity rather than that of us being spoiled by a pointless choice.

## Notes

1. Published in *Marie Claire*, September 1967, 42–44; *Oeuvres complètes* vol. 2, 413–16.

2. [Editors' note: 'Grande Mademoiselle' is a reference either to the sister of the seventeenth-century French king Louis XIV who was a 'Frondeuse' during the civil war of 1647–1653; and/or to those non-conformist women in early twentieth-century France, such as La Mistinguett, Charléty, Arletty, Sarah Bernhardt.]

# 12

# *A Case of Cultural Criticism*[1]

The town where these lines are being written is a small meeting place for hippies, mainly British, American and Dutch; they spend all day here in a very lively square in the old town, mixed in with (but not mixing with) the local population who, either through natural tolerance, amusement, habit or interest, accept them, exist alongside them and let them get on with life without ever understanding them or ever being surprised by them either. This gathering has certainly none of the density or diversity of the huge assemblies in San Francisco or New York; but, because hippyism in this place is out of its normal context, which is that of a rich and moralizing civilization, its usual meaning is fragmented; transplanted into a fairly poor country, and disoriented not by geographical but by economic and social exoticism (which is infinitely more divisive), here the hippy becomes contradictory (and no longer simply contrary), and this contradictoriness of the hippy is of interest to us because, on the level of social protest, it raises questions about the very link between the political and the cultural.

This contradictoriness is as follows. As an oppositional character, the hippy adopts a diametrically opposed position to the main values which underpin the way of life in the West (bourgeois, neo-bourgeois or petty bourgeois); the hippy knows full well that this way of life is one where materialism is central and it is consumption of goods that he aims to undermine. As far as food is concerned, the hippy rebels against mealtimes and menus (he eats very little, whenever and wherever) and rejects eating alone (when we eat in a group it is only ever done by simply adding extra individual portions, as symbolized now by the use of cloth or straw placemats which, gesturing towards the elegant, mark out the eating space of each guest; whereas the hippies, in Berkeley for example, have a collective cooking pot, communal cooking). As for accommodation, there is the same collectivism (one room for several people), as well as nomadism signalled by the bag, (that pouch) which the hippies have dangling around their long legs. Clothing (the outfit, should we say) is, as we know, a specific sign, the main choice made by the hippy; in relation to the norms in the West, there is a dual subversion, the elements of which sometimes go together: either there is absolutely manic fantasy, so as to transgress the *limits* of what is conventional to make this into a clear sign of that transgression itself (brocade trousers; draped jackets; long, white nightshirts; going barefoot even out on the street), or by borrowing overtly from ethnic costumes: djellabas, boubous, Hindu tunics, all nonetheless rendered other by some aberrant detail (necklaces, multicoloured and multi-layered neckbands etc.). Cleanliness (hygiene), the most important of American values (at least mythically), is counteracted in spectacular fashion: dirt on the body, in the hair, on the clothes; clothes dragging along the street, dusty feet, fair-haired babies playing in the gutter (but somehow it is still different from *real* dirtiness, different from a long-engrained poverty, from a dirtiness which *deforms* the body, the hand; hippy dirt is different, it has been borrowed for the holidays, sprinkled over like dust, and, like a footprint, not permanent). And finally, long hair on boys, their jewellery (necklaces, multiple rings, earrings), means that the sexes are becoming indistinguishable, not so much with a view to inverting gender identities but more so a process of removing them: what they are after, by switching between the normal features that distinguish between the sexes, is the neutral, i.e. a challenge to the 'natural' antagonism between the sexes.

We are not talking here about counter-values 'in your mind' by which the hippies put so much stock: drug use, withdrawal from the world, loss of aggression. It is quite clear that, if only in terms of making an impact, the hippies want to make a *reaction* political – clothing, accommodation, food, hygiene, sexuality are all made into *reactive* forces: this is meant in the Nietzschean sense; paradoxical as it may seem, the hippy (if only they would invest more intelligence into their adventure, their quest) could be one of the precursors to Nietzsche's 'superman' which he found in the ultimate nihilist, the one trying to widen and push forward the reactive value to the point of cutting off any chance of it being recuperated by some positive force or other. We know that Nietzsche pointed to two different incarnations of this nihilism, Christ and Buddha, and these two encapsulate the hippies' dreams: hippyism looks towards India (which is becoming the Mecca for the hippy movement) and many young hippies (too many for the phenomenon to go unnoticed) clearly want to have a Christ-like appearance – we are talking about symbols here, and not beliefs (the author of these lines saw a local crowd, with a markedly oriental vehemence, surround and threaten a young Christ with long hair and a pale face, accused of stealing a radio. It was unclear whether he was guilty, but he had perhaps fallen foul of the local *code* for what theft means: it was like a veritable evangelical tableau, a pious colour painting worthy of adorning a pastor's hallway). This is the direction hippies are taking and the signs they are sending out.

This direction, this meaning however (and it is what we discussed at the start) is recuperated by the context of the reality in which it has inevitably developed. In the United States, cultural contestation by the hippy is highly effective (we might say, a direct hit),[2] because it strikes *exactly* (in the sensitive places) at the good consciences of the well off, the guardians of social morals and of cleanliness: so hippyism is a stage (even if a rather short one) in cultural criticism which can be justified, because it paints the exact mirror image of the *American way of life*. But once out of its original context, hippy protest comes up against an enemy far more significant than American conformism, even if this is backed up by security on the university campus: poverty (where economics coyly uses the expression *developing countries*, culture and real life use the more honest *poverty*). This poverty *turns* the hippy's choice into a copy, a caricature of economic alienation, and this copy of poverty, though sported only lightly, becomes in fact distinctly irresponsible. For most traits invented by the hippy in opposition to his home civilization (a civilization of the rich) are the very ones which distinguish poverty, no longer as a sign, but much more severely as a clear indication, or an effect, on people's lives: undernourishment, collective living, bare feet, dirtiness, ragged clothing, are all forces which, in this context, are not there to be used in the symbolic fight against the world of riches but are the very forces against which we should be fighting. Symbols (which the hippy consumes frenetically) are therefore no longer reactive meanings, polemical forces, nor are they critical weapons that we appropriate from a well-off civilization that conceals its image of overnourishment by constant referral to it and that tries to make overnourishment's signifiers look glossy; if we think of them as being positive, these symbols become, not a *game*, or a higher form of symbolic activity, but a disguise, a lower form of cultural narcissism: as is demonstrated by linguistics, the context overturns the meaning, and the context here is that of economics.

So here is the dead end for a critique of culture that is cut off from its political argument. But what's the alternative? Could we conceive of a political critique of culture which is an active form of criticism and no longer a simply analytical or intellectual one, which would operate beyond the ideological conditioning by mass communications, in the very places, both subtle and diffuse, where the consumer is conditioned, precisely the places where the hippies play out their (incomplete) clairvoyance? Could we imagine a way of living that was, if not revolutionary, at least unobstructed? No one since Fourier has produced this image; no figure has yet been able to surmount and go beyond the militant and the hippy: the militant continues to live like a petty bourgeois, and the hippy like an *inverted* bourgeois; between these two, nothing. The political critique and the cultural critique don't seem to be able to coincide.

## Notes

1. Published in *Communications* 14 (Nov.) 1969, 97–99; *Oeuvres complètes* vol. 2, 544–46.

2. [Editors' note: there seems to be a play on words here by Barthes – 'droite' could mean both 'direct' or 'right wing'.]

# 13

# *Showing How Rhetoric Works*[1]

## *Writing of Fashion*

It is clear that Fashion utterances are entirely derived not from a style but a writing; by describing an item of clothing, or how it is worn, the writer/journalist invests in his words nothing of himself [sic] nor of his psychology; he simply conforms *to a certain conventional and regulated style* (we might say an *ethos*), which furthermore announces immediately that it is from a Fashion magazine.

## *Fashion Ideology*

On the rhetorical level there is a signified that corresponds to the writing of Fashion, which is Fashion ideology.

The world aimed at by written Fashion *ignores opposites*, ... one can be presented with two apparently *contradictory* characteristics between which there is nothing that requires making a choice.

## *Fashion Text*

As Fashion is a phenomenon of initiation, its wording naturally plays a didactic role: the Fashion text represents in some way *the authoritative wording* of someone who knows everything that is behind the confused, or incomplete, appearance of the visible forms; this wording therefore constitutes the moment when what is hidden becomes visible, in which one can almost see, in a secularized form, the sacred halo of *divinatory texts*; all the more since the knowledge of Fashion never comes without a price; it holds a sanction for those who are excluded from it: the stigma of being *unfashionable.*

## Pseudo-syntax

Indeed, without leaving behind the actual line of the words (since this guarantees the meaning of an item of clothing), we can try and replace the grammatical links (which themselves are charged with no vestimentary meaning) with a *pseudo-syntax*, whose articulations, removed from grammar, will have the sole aim of making manifest a *vestimentary meaning,* and *no longer* something to be understood within discourse.

## The Support for Meaning in Fashion

Materiality, *inertia* and *conductivity* all make the support for meaning into an original element in the Fashion system, at least in relation to language. Indeed, language has nothing about it which would resemble a support for meaning (...) so one cannot divide the linguistic syntagm into active, meaningful elements and inert, meaningless elements: in language everything means. The necessity and originality of the support for meaning reside precisely in the fact that clothing is not *in itself* a system of meaning, as language is; in terms of substance, the support represents the materiality of the item of clothing, *as it* exists *outside* of any *process of meaning.*

## Rhetoric of the Observation of Fact

Fashion sits at the crossroads between chance and divine decree: its decisions become a self-evident fact. All Fashion then has to do is practise a rhetoric of pure observation of fact (*loose dresses are in*), and all the fashion magazine has to do is report *what is* ('we can see the camelhair sweater coming back'), even if, like a wise historian, it knows how to discern in a simple event the way the whole market is moving (*The Fashion for black-dyed mink is growing*). By making

Fashion into an inevitable force, the magazine imparts to it all the ambiguity of an object *without cause*, but not one without will.

## *Fashion Trajectory*

A fashion is recorded at the very moment it is announced, the very moment it is prescribed. The whole of Fashion rhetoric is contained in this shortcut: *stating that which is being imposed*; producing Fashion and then seeing in it nothing but an *effect without a named cause*; then retaining from this effect only the phenomenon; and finally leaving this phenomenon to develop as if its life depended solely upon itself: such is the trajectory that fashion follows so as to convert its cause, its law and its signs all at once into fact.

## *Fashion Infidelity*

All new Fashion is a refusal to inherit, a subversion of the oppression left by the preceding Fashion. Fashion experiences itself as a Right, the natural right of the present over the past; defined by its very infidelity, Fashion nevertheless lives in *a world which it wants to come into being and which it sees as ideally stable,* a world shot through with glances that are conformist.

## *Fashion Dogmatism*

Fashion's aggressiveness, whose rhythm can even be one of *vendettas*, ends up itself being undone by a more patient image of time; by that *absolute, dogmatic, vengeful present tense* in which Fashion speaks.

## *Closed System*

The present tense of Fashion becomes here the guarantee of the system's declared arbitrariness: this system tends to enclose its synchronic dimension more and more, as each year and in a flash it *goes completely into reverse* and collapses into the nothingness of the past.

## *Fashion Neurosis*

Each of these *todays* is a triumphant structure whose order is extensive with (or alien to) time in such a way that Fashion tames the new even before producing it and so accomplishes that paradox in which the 'new' is both unpredictable and yet already decreed.

Thus, with long-term memory abolished and with time reduced to the duo of that which is rejected and that which is inaugurated, pure Fashion, logical Fashion is never anything other than the *amnesiac substitution* of the present for the past. We could almost speak of a *Fashion neurosis*.

## *Note*

1. Published in *Change* 4 (1969), 106–9. [Editors' note: adapted from *The Fashion System*, as translated by Matthew Ward and Richard Howard, London, Jonathan Cape, 1985.]

# Clothes, Fashion and System in the Writings of Roland Barthes: 'Something Out of Nothing'

*by Andy Stafford*

Although men have otherwise no right to talk about fashion in clothes, the sort of materials, trimmings, cut, and all the other details, nevertheless research has provided a more respectable reason for treating these trivialities as important, and discussing them at length, than what women are allowed to have in this field.

*G. W. F. Hegel*

Clothes only relate to their opposites.

*Karl Marx*

[U]topia occupies, as it should, an intermediary position between the praxis of the poor and that of the rich.

*Roland Barthes*

## Introduction

It is perhaps surprising that the novelist and writer Alison Lurie, in a later edition of her study *The Language of Clothes*, should maintain the following comment: 'Sociologists tell us that fashion too is a language of signs ... and Roland Barthes ... speaks of theatrical dress as a kind of writing ... None of these theorists, however, have gone on to remark what seems obvious: that if clothing is a language it must have a vocabulary and a grammar like other languages' (1992: 3–4). Roland Barthes's *The Fashion System* (published in France in 1967) was first translated into English in 1985, and should have provided Lurie's second edition with ample evidence of Barthes's thesis: that fashion, as a 'written' phenomenon, does have a vocabulary and a grammar, and this is precisely what his *Fashion System* set out to analyse. Indeed, as this collection of Barthes's writings on fashion theory shows, the form that clothes have taken in general was swiftly compared by Barthes to a form of language. In fact Barthes was one of the first to deploy semiology – originally conceived by the Swiss linguist Ferdinand de Saussure at the start of the twentieth century as a branch of linguistics – to the study of fashion; and it could be argued furthermore that it was his use of semiological method – the division of the means of communication between humans into signs, and then into the sign's constituent parts, the signifier and the signified – that was bound to lead to his view that fashion was a language, with a vocabulary and a grammar.

So Lurie's comment is a rather irrelevant one, even if, as has been hinted, *The Fashion System* 'is *the* most boring book ever written about fashion' (Moeran 2004: 36). What is at stake then in Barthes's work on fashion is the extent to which his 'linguistic-semiological' analysis is successful. Olivier Burgelin, former collaborator of Barthes's for the journal *Communications* and an early listener to Barthes's views on clothing in 1959 (Calvet 1994: 132), wrote provocatively in relation to the *Fashion System*: 'with brutal inelegance', hadn't Barthes 'taken 300 pages to write his monumental but indigestible analysis and whose "ideological payback" was not palpably higher than that of *Mythologies*, where he had taken three pages to get each of his points across?' (1974: 16). But Burgelin was not about to break off his friendship with Barthes with such a comment. At the same time – and this is the sense of Burgelin's 'double' view of Barthes's ambiguous relationship to fashion – Burgelin recognized that Barthes's journey from *Mythologies* in 1957 was considerable: 'He has situated himself in relation to Fashion', Burgelin concluded, 'in such a way that was radically new and which remains impregnably original' (16).

It is this contradiction which sits at the heart of Barthes's writing on fashion. On the one hand, *The Fashion System* can appear turgid, heavy, long, too methodical, even rebarbative (Carter 2003: 144); on the other, it is a crucial and repeatedly useful reference point for any theorization of fashion worth its salt. This contradiction explains perhaps why there has been so little secondary criticism of *The Fashion System* in the English-speaking world since Barthes's death in 1980 and the explosion of interest across the 1980s and 1990s in his writings other than *The Fashion System*.[1] And if *The Fashion System* has been overlooked in Barthes's oeuvre, then there is a further paradox. Like much of Barthes's theory, his writing on fashion seems to percolate slowly, in fragmentary form, into fashion theory; it is regularly cited, incidentally, here and there; and yet it is not treated as a body of writing. This has much to do, I am sure, with the 'postmodern' spirit of the last two decades of the twentieth century; and perhaps now, with the dust beginning to settle on postmodernism, is a propitious moment in which to begin an assessment of Barthes's fashion theory. In this essay, therefore, I hope to show how Barthes moves across the 1960s, from his earliest work on clothes in the late 1950s to his growing fascination with the body in the early 1970s. We will look specifically then at the passage from his 'high structuralism' of 1966 (exemplified by 'An Introduction to the Structural Analysis of Narratives', Sontag 1982) to the more sceptical use of structuralism in his *S/Z* of 1970, which was tantamount to a 'mutation', a 'rupture': in short, how he moved from structuralism to post-structuralism. It is this move from seeing fashion as major social object of French mass culture to deeming fashion to be essentially 'empty' that we will set out to explore. How could Barthes at one stage consider this innocuous social obligation – to cover the body – as part of a wider social signification with a fullness of human meaning, and then relegate this phenomenon to the status of *legerdemain,* a form of trickery? It is possible that working from 1957 to 1969 on clothing, against left-wing intellectual norms, Barthes finally ended up agreeing with those who had originally been suspicious of his work. But, as with all of Barthes's thought, it is firstly a question of how he gets to this position; and secondly where it subsequently leads him. It would not then be unreasonable to consider Barthes's work on fashion under his favoured figure of the spiral: Barthes ends up in 1969 where he should have been in 1957, but further along the spiral.

Michael Carter has suggested already the influence of Barthes on fashion theory in general (2003, chapter 8), building brilliantly up to this in his collection of essays on fashion and clothes theorists. He suggests (152) that the early writings might provide a much more rounded view of clothing in Barthes's thought. As we stated in the editors' note, however, it is important to unpack this area of study, and it is precisely Barthes's trajectory across the years 1957 to 1969 that allows us to do this. This book stops at the more militant, surprising Barthes (see his 1969 interview with John Whitley), when it is *S/Z* (1970), his terroristic reading of a Balzac short story, that inaugurates a new phase in Barthes's politico-theoretical career, but not before he has dealt a subtle but distinctly sharp critique of hippies and hippy fashion, in the 1969 article that closes our anthology. Clearly, the thirteen very varied pieces collected in this book represent a body of writing and research emerging across a dramatic twelve-year period in France's cultural and political history (and are, by mere coincidence, roughly coterminous with General de Gaulle's period as French president). And yet they also show a Barthes in intense theorization of both the form and the content of his own work, applying new theories from inside (and more commonly outside) fashion and clothing theory. These two roles – theorist and 'product' of his time, that of the structuralist (over)determined by system and that of the existentialist in voluntarist opposition to capitalism's social structures – meet in the figure and the writing praxis of the 'essayist'.

'Something out of nothing' is how Barthes characterized his achievement in an interview at the time of publication: *The Fashion System* was a 'poetic project' because the semiologist had made an object out of something that, if not entirely empty, had been 'of great frivolity and no importance' (1985b, 67). In other words, said Barthes, here was the importance of the 'void', of emptiness, that had begun to dominate Western societies and which Mallarmé had been first to valorize: 'the passion for meaning' in which *The Fashion System* was engaged found itself 'in exemplary fashion in objects which were very close to being nothing' (ibid.). Barthes was thus acutely aware of the power, responsibility but also aesthetic choices of the critic-writer, the *écrivain* over the *écrivant* – and this was brilliantly illustrated in his polemical 1966 essay on the role of the literary critic, *Criticism and Truth*. But what did this mean when it came to the critic confronted with fashion and clothing? This is precisely the essayist's (even the essay's) very wager: to systematize the world in a form that is aesthetic yet responsible, playful yet grown-up, questioning but mindful of closure (mindful of closure but still questioning, if you like), distant but still political.

Thus Barthes was asking very pertinent questions about human society. Maybe, if Chomsky was right about humanity's innate ability to generate grammar, then there was also, Barthes was suggesting, an innate human tendency towards literature, narrative, stories (Sontag 1982: 251–52). For an understanding of fashion – if taken as a language – this suggestion is crucial: we are innately *obliged* to narrate clothing forms either verbally or mentally; if we do not do this when thinking about clothing, especially fashion, then a magazine, an advert, a friend, a shopworker, whatever, will do it for us. 'It is impossible to consider a cultural object outside the articulated, spoken and written language which surrounds it', Barthes opined in 1967 (1985b: 65). It is precisely this idea – that verbalizing the real, or our desires, is a core human activity, especially when we are confronted with daily objects in human society – that may become one of the key theories linked to the name of Roland Barthes. In fashion, it justifies Barthes's concentration on the written or 'represented' garment (Carter 2003: 149–152), *pace* the anti-intellectualism of a clothes designer such as Ian Griffiths (White/Griffiths 2000: 78–79). And therefore the view that we constantly verbalize the real helps also to go beyond a mere 'reflection' theory of fashion whereby a person is shown simply to reflect their personality/psychology/social standing in their appearance (Carter 152), and to look for a more subtle, 'refractive' view of fashion which incorporates the *im*personalist manner in which form influences taste. In this impersonalist schema, the romantic notion of 'inspiration', in everything, from literature to fashion, was anathema to Barthes in ascendant scientific mode. However, it cannot be stressed enough that his interest in finding a scientific understanding of fashion form is always dependent on the essayist's obedience to provisionality. And here Barthes was at the cutting edge of avant-garde theories of fashion, though, curiously, he wrote precious little on avant-garde fashion itself, despite the abundance of examples in the modern period (see Stern 2004). Furthermore, it is worth pointing out that Fashion has interested the avant-garde throughout the nineteenth and twentieth centuries in France. This is not just in the work of Stéphane Mallarmé, to whose late nineteenth-century fashion writing Barthes's work has deep affinities (see Furbank/Cain's introduction to Mallarmé 2004: 10), but also in the radical film-making of one Jean-Luc Godard in the 1988 film about the catwalk *On s'est tous défilé* (see Temple 1999). And so it is to precursors in Barthes's work that we must first turn.

## *Precursors to Theorizing Fashion: The Labyrinth*

In his final lectures at the Collège de France in Paris just before his death in 1980, and concluding a collaborative set of lectures on 'the Labyrinth' (2003: 177), Barthes felt in a position to come clean about his work on clothing and what he thought of the subject itself. He describes how, in 1953 or 1954, he had met up with the philosopher Maurice Merleau-Ponty to discuss work on a semiology of clothing. Quoting Merleau-Ponty, Barthes remembered a phrase from the discussion: clothing was a 'faux bon sujet' (false good topic). Applying this description to the Labyrinth as metaphor, he suggests that a 'false good topic' is one which exhausts itself or is exhausted from the start, which forces the topic's 'development' to be a repetition of the subject-word. In fine Barthes style, he illustrated this with a tautology: 'The Labyrinth is a Labyrinth'.

The paradox of Barthes's work on clothing and fashion is, then, a fine paradox: how to research and write on a subject that, at best, has nothing to be said about it, and at worst invites pure tautology. This is an essayistic challenge typical of Barthes. He then goes on to say why the Labyrinth is a 'false good topic' in ways which we could continue to apply to clothing. Firstly, it is a form which is so well designed that anything said about it appears to be *within* (*'en deçà'*) the form itself; 'the topic is richer than the general, the denotation than the connotation, the letter than the symbol'; there is nothing to understand in a Labyrinth, it cannot be summarized. Secondly, as a metaphor, the Labyrinth is everywhere in human society (monuments, gardens, games, cities, tricks, the brain) thereby losing its metaphorical specificity: in the Labyrinth 'metaphorical power is at once applicable to everything but also poor'. Barthes attributed the poverty of the Labyrinth metaphor to the 'pregnancy of the story, of the myth' and his interest in the Labyrinth metaphor is attached then not to what a Labyrinth is, or to how many are there, nor even to how to get out, but to the question of where a Labyrinth begins. This attentiveness to the 'viscosity of forms', to 'progressive consistencies', thresholds, intensities, reflects an interest in liminality that is crucial to his work on clothing – for example, 'Where does clothing begin?' or 'Where does clothing end?'

Barthes applied a deeply Hegelian sensibility to change and structure, the very dualistic being of Form, to a subject which is both ubiquitous and yet impoverished in its social existence. 'Clothing is what we clothe ourselves in', would perhaps be the relevant Barthesian tautology. And yet, not only are the combinations and productions of clothing forms all around us, discussed, designed, purchased and then deemed finished, but also clothing is potentially the most basic of human forms of communication. It is this dialectic between richness/ubiquity and banality/caducity that underpins Barthes's work on apparel. It is here perhaps that we find the ultimate strength of Barthesian theory of fashion. As with his writings on literature, on petty bourgeois ideology, on historiography, Barthes comes closest to being able to be both inside *and* outside Form and we will make some tentative conclusions on the politics of form at the end of this essay. It would appear that Barthes wishes to sit happily at once in the deeply critical, pessimistic camp – represented by Lefebvre, the early Baudrillard, Perec or the Situationists – for whom fashion is a commodity, a 'constraint', and where fetishism rules supreme

– but then also to sit in the more optimistic, 'appropriation' camp – represented by Lipovetsky (1994 [1987]), later Baudrillard, Certeau and Maffesoli – where fashion can be seen to represent positive and potentially democratic options.[2]

It is the contention of this essay, then, that it is precisely Barthes's formalism, that is his sensitivity to Form, from the 'inside' as much from the 'outside', which allows him to straddle and swing between these radically insuperable differences of opinion. So, just as Barthes suggested that it is futile to search for the 'origins' of fashion and was not asserting the importance of human communication to the wearing of clothes in order then to reassign a new fundamental origin to clothing, it is then perhaps just as futile to look for a key moment or phenomenon, a primal object, which urges Barthes to look at clothing. However, a number of contributing circumstances can be more accurately located, of which personal circumstances were the first.

Barthes found himself, for various reasons including illness, without a career in the 1950s but at the same time was interested in the growth of sociology and a participant in the burgeoning popular theatre movement. Needless to say, clothing, or 'costume' as they say in French with all its theatrical connotations, was bound to be a starting point. Having written on theatre costumes for the popular theatre movement, and having also regretted the way hairstyles seemed to be dictated to people by the growth of the cinema star – see 'Visages et figures' (1953/1993a) – Barthes was invited by Georges Friedmann in 1955 to work with his friend Edgar Morin on the history of work clothes. Nothing came of this or seems to remain of this work, though there are important sections in *The Fashion System* on 'work' clothes within fashion (see chapter 18) where Barthes notes how some fashions gesture towards the image of work as a sign ultimately of leisure.[3] It is here that Barthes's systematic study of clothing began. Already, in a number of lesser-known mythological studies from the mid-1950s, he had spoken of the 'endimanchement' (Sunday-besting) of the child in the clothing worn in advertising features, suggesting that the instigation of a 'Sunday best' ideology was a crucial function of children's clothing (see 'Enfant-copies', 1993b [1955], 461–62). However, another, earlier friendship had perhaps helped Barthes into the world of clothing.

Introduced to Algirdas Julien Greimas (known as 'Guy') in Egypt in the late 1940s, Barthes was quickly influenced by his knowledge of Saussure, Jakobson and Brøndal (Calvet 1994: 94–95). Greimas had recently been awarded his doctorate in Paris, which at that time required a main thesis and a *thèse secondaire*. The main thesis was on the language of fashion in 1830, using fashion publications from the period, and the second went on to show how social life in the France of 1830 was reflected in this vocabulary.[4] Greimas was to go on to become one of France's most important semiologists and his 1955 article commemorating the fortieth anniversary of Saussure's *Course in General Linguistics* is an important statement of the contemporary applicability of Saussurian method.[5] Indeed, Greimas is a constant reference point for Barthes's work on Saussure and semiology.[6] It is even suggested (Greimas 2000: 'Arrivé', xii) that Greimas got bored with fashion and passed the job on to Barthes.[7]

The final element of the conjuncture in which Barthes began to work on clothing was the growth of the 'new novel' in France. The rich beginning of Barthes's 1961 essay 'From Gemstones to Jewellery' (see chapter 5 here), which considers the hard, objectified nature of the origins of gemstones and their mythical appeal, seems strongly redolent of Barthes's early championing of the *nouveau roman* in the 1950s, especially in relation to Jean Cayrol and Alain Robbe-Grillet. In the *nouveau roman* Barthes championed in particular its 'chosisme' (thingism). Objects or things in literature, suggested Barthes, could be a reminder of humanity's 'station' in a post-holocaust, post-Einsteinian, mass communication world where consumerism tended to invest in objects a widespread mythic status. Literary 'chosisme' was a counterbalance to an incipient anthropomorphism, because it denied the pathetic fallacy or commodity fetishism with which we tended to invest objects around us. 'Chosisme' also fitted with the growing interest in structuralism of the mid-1950s where inanimate objects were matt, meaningless, paradoxically transparent, in stark contrast to human objects; but these inanimate objects were swiftly contaminated by the meaning-making machine of human society of communication and expression. In good structural terms, to posit a world where objects just *are* was not only a view reminiscent of Sartre's description in *Nausea* of the experience of the facticity of 'things'. To invoke the simple 'thereness' of objects was also in opposition to humanity's inability in a social situation (that is, where there is more than one person) to avoid meaning, whether created actively or passively. This had an important bearing on clothing and human appearance in general.

If, in Sartrian terms, we only exist for the 'other', then, by golly, the individual will do it to the best of their ability by sending out, continuously, self-confirming radar signals, bouncing them like bats off other animate objects in order to find their way. In this 'impersonalist' view of human identity, the Other (others) are mere sounding boards, mirrors for each of our attempts to affirm and confirm our characters which are increasingly perceived as multivalent. The problem for an individualist impersonalism is that *everyone*, that is all of those 'others' who are 'confirming' our individual existence, are all *also* doing exactly the same. Everyone is reflecting themselves in everyone else. Of course, if everyone is doing the same, then the various dimensions to our identity are spread across the entire sum of those people known to each of us and whose identities are in turn *also* refracted across the whole sum and so on. In other words, not only was the human subject's identity located (or decentred) in anyone encountered by that subject, but also human identity 'escaped' into the metabolic circuits of human society where it lay beyond the control of either the individual or the collective. This was a central element in any understanding of fashion; as one critic has put it: 'Fashion ... flatters the universal desire for identity together with the no less universal desire to be a multiplicity of persons' (Lavers 1982: 161).

As with Kroeber (Carter 2003: 91), Barthes was not interested in a simplistic 'reflection' theory in his account of clothing and fashion.[8] In a dialectic with no origins, a dialogue between the human individual and the 'super-organic' – via decentred self-perception in the eyes of others, themselves in the same position – the self (as multiple selves) negotiates its complex and multiple self-reflections. This was not simply an Hegelian, narcissistic view of self caught in a complex web, but a new development in mass human society dominated more and more by the image (in photographs, cinema and television), which went so far in Western society that humanity had, in Barthes's words, 'lost its face' ([1953] 1993a). It is not surprising then that structuralism – at least in its French version

– would grow out of a literary aesthetic such as the *nouveau roman* which challenged all notions of reflection, would look to 'primitive' societies (discussed in the work of Lévi-Strauss) for explanations behind humanity's trajectory and would increasingly deploy a critique of those Western values that seemed incapable or unwilling to reflect upon a crisis of reflection, upon humanity's infinitely irrelevant place in the universe. The inanimate (non-human) then paradoxically took on the warmth of authenticity but thereby ran the risk of re-romanticizing – in a spiral – the inhuman with human qualities. In fact structuralism has been described as a form of anti-humanism but like the *nouveau roman* it wanted mainly to question, decentre, our emotional and affective investment in the inhuman and the inanimate. Here Fashion and clothing rules were an excellent example not only of this decentred, 'super-organic' and complex world of mass communications but also of just how important language ('taste' in all senses) was to maintaining society's equilibrium and functioning – what Carter calls, in his discussion of Thorstein Veblen, the 'collective, authorless social process' (2003: 49). This radical questioning and decentring in 1950s thought also had its counterpart in historical enquiry.

Though not strictly speaking 'structuralist', the group of historians and social theorists gathered around the journal *Annales* was trying to renew historical and social studies by urging it to take into account the conflicting categories of 'event' and 'structure'. Against historicizing history, its main theorist Lucien Febvre wanted a historical phenomenon to be studied in relation to its milieu by paying regard to the links that made up a more general 'collective mentality' in the past, what he called 'the mental baggage of an epoch'. Barthes borrowed this idea for his work on France's classical playwright Racine (see 1992 [1963]: 157, published originally in *Annales* in 1960), in which he asserted that literary history must be sociological, looking at activities and institutions, not individuals. This link between form and institution was then inverted by Barthes and smoothly reapplied to clothing history. Furthermore, sensitive to Febvre's argument of 'periodising' historical trends, where Febvre argues for a human-centred and equilibrium-sensitive form of historical dating (see chapter 1, note 9 in this book), Barthes became beholden also to Braudel's 'longue durée' theory of social history, which provides us with a clear link to Kroeber's 'super-organic' view of social change (Carter 2003: 96 n. 38).[9]

This aspect of Barthes's early work on clothing has been a key influence on (French-speaking) fashion theorists. His view that the most important thing is 'the tendency of every corporeal cover to insert itself into a formal, organized, normative system recognized by society' (see chapter 1 here) has subsequently been used by Margerie, Poulenc, Davray-Piékolek and Guillaume in their chapter on ornamentation, to suggest how religiosity and transgression led to exclusion (in Klopp 1991: 143). Similarly, Philippe Perrot (1994) quotes Barthes's 1957 article on clothing history, almost verbatim, when considering how difficult it is to track and explain clothing 'form' in history.[10] This influence is, however, much more to do with an *Annales*-inspired social history than with a structuralist view of fashion per se. Therefore, the danger of losing the subject in history, as structuralism is frequently accused of doing, does not have its roots (with regard to Barthes's early work on clothing at least) in Febvre's or the *Annales* view of history. After all, Febvre's historical work is fundamentally concerned with the *vécu* (lived experience) of human actants in the past. Then again, Barthes is also influenced by Gurvitch's Durkheimian conception of sociology, which aimed to get beyond considering society as merely the sum of its individuals. So, by being dialectical in its notion of a social totality, his 'historical sociology', dependent on a tight Gurvitchian 'total' sociology and an *Annales*-inspired attention to the *vécu* was to become the basis of Barthes's social psychology of fashion. If Barthes the structuralist is rightly accused of ignoring the 'subject in history', ironically this phase of his career was coincidental with a desire for a total and subjective understanding of humans' interest in fashion. To consider this paradox further, we must look at the competing epistemologies to explain the theoretical moves Barthes made across the 1960s.

Before doing this, it is worth pointing out the limits of my analysis here. Within Barthes's work on clothing and fashion, there are competing spheres of interest – the body, theatre, photography – that we will not have time to explore. Clothing was clearly an important concern for a popular theatre activist keen to point to the 'Illnesses in theatre costumes' – an article he wrote in 1955 (1972 [1964]) which were holding back a truly people's theatre and Barthes divided the 'thought-out' theatre costume into the 'healthy' and the folkloric and 'unthought-out' costume into the 'ill'. The body was also a key component in his work on theatre as much as on myth, literature and historiography and the body and theatre costumes meet in his commentary on photography of a production of a Brecht play in 1960.[11] And, obviously, Barthes's clothing and fashion writings – and not just *The Fashion System* – are radically concerned with how the body is made to signify via apparel. So his work on clothing was bound to bring back an optic that he had explored in 'Visages et figures' in 1953: namely that the body, not just the face, is alienated by its 'writing' of fashion via a system (just like literature or dramaturgy) that is stereotyped, not thought out ('pensé'). This is the body not as instinct but as writing, an optic which finds its utopian dimension in his 1971 book *Sade, Fourier, Loyola*.[12] This discrimination of clothes from the body notwithstanding, the link between the body and clothing in Barthes's thought will return in the discussion of Hegel at the conclusion of this essay.

## *The Three S's: Sociology, Semiology, Structuralism*

Modern democratic society has made fashion into a sort of crosssubsidising organism, destined to establish an automatic equilibrium between the demand for singularity and the right for all to have it.

*Roland Barthes in 'Dandyism and Fashion'*

There is far more to the relationship between semiology and structuralism than merely historical conjuncture. Both borrow heavily from Saussurianism. Both mobilize the key human paradox that social and human phenomena, in the manner in which they act as 'communicators' between humans, combine the arbitrariness of form with the rigour of context. Indeed, it seems to us now that structuralist theory obscured semiology throughout the 1960s through the debates (especially with Marxism) around the notion of human agency. It was only when structuralism was perceived as compromised by the events of May 1968 in France that semiology could re-emerge, albeit with the new name of 'semiotics'. Though still using Saussurian differential philosophy after May 1968, semiotics was a far more *corrosive* form of social research than semiology or structuralism, keen to distance itself from any technocratic or positivist uses ascribed to structuralism, and 'terroristic' in its application to Western thought, be it in the hands of a Derrida or a Lacan. Semiotics emerged then out of *post*-structuralism. However, as the name 'post-structuralism' suggests, there were elements of structuralism maintained within it and it is simplistic to suggest that post-structuralism simply swept away its structuralist forerunner. By the same token, it is dangerous to subsume semiology within structuralism. On the one hand, it is premature to consider Barthes's deployment of semiology in *Mythologies* as 'structuralist'. On the other hand, it would be churlish to divorce semiology and structuralism. In this section, we will look then at how semiology competed with structuralism in Barthes's writing on fashion, but also how within this competition small signs of the later *post*-structuralist practices could be seen emerging well *before* the seismic epistemological and political changes of May 1968.

Semiology came before structuralism in Barthes's work. In fact Barthes's 'structuralist' phase did not really start properly until his work on Racine in 1960. According to Calvet (1973: 82) the 'differential' turn that Barthesian semiology was taking between *Elements of Semiology* and *The Fashion System* was operated by his use of Trubetskoy's phonology, based rigorously as this was on a 'differential' taxonomy. This, says Calvet (81), appeared most clearly in Barthes's 1963 piece 'The Structuralist Activity' (Barthes 1972) where for the first time he looked at the sign in a 'differential' way.

However, the chronology is not as simple as might appear. Clearly, the decision as early as 1959 to look at fashion as written (or verbalized) clothing, as opposed to actually worn clothing, was an important factor in this shift to seeing society based on language, here exemplified by fashion. But we must remember that Barthes's structuralist analysis of narratives did not appear until 1966. Unaware, it seems, that Barthes had already mentioned Trubetskoy's work on phonology and clothes in 1957 and in 1959 (see chapters 1 and 2 in this book), Calvet (1973: 83) is keen to suggest that an important shift does indeed take place in Barthes's thought around 1962. Whereas

Barthes's theoretical essay concluding *Mythologies*, 'Myth Today', had concentrated on Saussurian notions of the sign, nowhere did it look at the 'paradigmatic', or 'differential', dimension of signs (83). Barthesian semiology (especially of fashion) understood its object in systemic or 'structural' fashion but this was a parallel, rather than a subsumable, effect of structural analyses. This point is made obliquely by the left-wing critic Tom Nairn in his review of *The Fashion System* for *The New Statesmen* in 1967. For Nairn, *The Fashion System* is an 'aberration'. Not only did Barthes miss the material, substantial reality of clothes within fashion – 'A fashion cannot be born without being named', Nairn agreed with Barthes, but 'it is not born *only* by being named'; Barthes had also seemingly abandoned his semiological analysis by swaying towards structuralism. Whereas Barthes's semiology had shown that meaning *is* relationship, his more 'structuralist' phase, argued Nairn, was now insisting upon language as 'separation, analysis'. Barthes's structuralist approach in *The Fashion System*, complained Nairn, was operating 'the sifting out of an elusive reality from ambiguous appearances'; thus *The Fashion System* was far too 'formalist' for Nairn's liking. As evidence of Nairn's and Calvet's critiques of Barthes's mixing of structuralism into semiology, the preface to *The Fashion System* suggested that Saussure's belief that linguistics was merely a branch of semiology, the general science of culture, should be inverted: semiology, Barthes hinted in 1967, was merely a branch of linguistics, linguistics being not just a model of meaning in human society but the fundamental basis of human society. This is a crucial moment in the confusion of semiology with structuralism, indeed of the subsuming of semiology into a differential and paradigmatic form of analysis known as structuralism. Crucial in inspiring Barthes's more formalist and structuralist activity of the mid-1960s was the publication in France of Jakobson's *Essais de linguistique générale* in 1963 and Tzvetan Todorov's edited anthology of Russian formalism, *Théorie de la littérature* in 1965, both of which crystallized a more 'differential' structuralist phase of Barthes's work, and which is found (to Nairn's dismay) in *The Fashion System*.

Therefore Barthes's strictly 'structuralist' phase proper began somewhere between 1960 (with the work on Racine) and 1964, and therefore his pivotal decision in 1959 to look at the language of fashion (rather than clothing history) was based on other factors. Moreover, it has not been insisted upon enough that the total disregard for worn clothing, in favour of written (or verbalized, 'represented') and illustrated clothing forms, is a fine example of Barthes's interest in the image/text interface. Although Jakobson is not mentioned in Barthes's 1961 article 'The Photographic Message' (Sontag 1982: 194–210), in which the relationship between text and image is a central part of the analysis, Barthes was already anticipating Jakobson's notion of the *shifter* (see Jakobson 1990: 386–392).[13] It was the shifter ('look', 'here we have', 'there', etc.) that is the crucial 'clutch' – to borrow Jakobson's metaphor, hijacked and redeployed by Barthes according to Calvet (1973: 91) – which smoothes the passage between written text and image; it is a part of speech that will be central to Barthes's subsequent work on the written, 'represented' fashion in *The Fashion System* (Barthes 1985a: 6).[14]

'Language and Clothing' (chapter 2 here) then becomes a pivotal text, before his structuralist activity proper, in the move from studying clothing history to looking at contemporary fashion. Perhaps not surprisingly, given the success of *Mythologies* in 1957, Barthes was quick in the article's conclusion to make the link between fashion and mythology. But this comes at the end of an important discussion where he seemed to abandon the study of clothes and the history of their forms. Does Barthes decide to move from clothing to fashion – as we see at the end of this article – *because* the task of working on clothing would require a 'vast information apparatus' or because, as soon as one tries to break down meaning in clothes it, like literature, 'tends to evaporate'? Or both? Or was the influence of structuralism now irresistible?

One answer comes in the famous 1971 interview in *Tel Quel*: 'I originally intended to perform a proper socio-semiology of Clothing, of all Clothing (I had even done a bit of research on this); then, following a private remark by Lévi-Strauss, I decided to homogenize the corpus and restrict myself to *written* clothing (as described in fashion magazines)' (Barthes 1971, 99). This explained in part the lateness with which *The Fashion System* was finally published seeing as, by all accounts, it was finished by 1963. Barthes also seemed to be suggesting in 1971 that even though '"Blue is in Fashion This Year"', published in 1960, used the exact methodology finally deployed in *The Fashion System* in 1967, this methodology was actually only part of the original plan which was to cover the whole of clothing and not just (written) fashion as found in fashion magazines. This then makes the early preface to *The Fashion System* (included in this book, chapter 7) also pivotal, but pivotal not so much to the move from clothing history to fashion system (this, as we have seen, seemed to take place around 1959–60), but in relation to how to present semiology given the rise of structuralism. In other words, Barthes discarded this early preface, waited four years whilst working within his new structuralist, 'differential' sensibility – as evident in *Elements of Semiology* and then in his 'Introduction to the Structural Analysis of Narrative' – before then recasting the precise significance of what he was doing in *The Fashion System* in applying semiology to written fashion.

The crucial difference between the early preface and the final version of the preface to *The Fashion System* then seems to hinge on the 'semiology as part of linguistics' inversion that Barthes operated on Saussure's original formulation, which had proposed that linguistics be merely a part of a much wider science of signs that is semiology. This is indeed hinted at in the opening paragraphs of the early preface, but never once stated in the bold terms that we find in *Elements of Semiology* and in the final preface to *The Fashion System*, and which was then to so dismay the linguisticians Mounin and Martinet.

We can see once again then that structuralism 'intervened' between 1963 and 1967, both to obscure (but not deny) semiology, and to recast (but not leave untainted) the semiological project. This also leads us to suggest that Calvet's justification for inverting his analysis of *The Fashion System* and *Elements of Semiology* (1973: 115) – based on his theory that *The Fashion System* was basically all set up and ready to run *before* Barthes published *Elements of Semiology* in 1964 – was perhaps a little hasty, in that it does not allow for a slow gestation of the method and theories of *The Fashion System* across the whole ten-year period 1957–67 (it also suggests that the early preface to *The Fashion System* could be considered as a first stab at the *Elements of Semiology*). That said, Calvet's suggestion that *The Fashion System* was done and dusted before *Elements of Semiology* was published in 1964 is actually felicitous in that it allows us to see how important the work on clothing history between 1957 to 1959 actually was for his subsequent semiological analyses. Thus Barthes appears in the early preface to be highly sensitive to the dangers of turning semiology into a sociology, that is of making semiology into a critique of ideology; and thereby he was pre-empting (but unfortunately for him this pre-empting remained unpublished) the critiques of Mounin, of Prieto, of Molino, of Martinet, and displaying a sensitivity which is turned into a virtue in the foreword to *The Fashion System*. In promoting linguistics *over* semiology Barthes was now clearly adopting a structuralist point of view. At the same time however, he was slightly embarrassed by the scientism and the naivety of believing that one could simply apply semiology, without any problem, as a meta-language, to fashion, to the city, to food. This was to be an important *post*-structuralist critique of structuralism's scientism that was to come to the fore in the turmoil of May 1968, and a critique that allowed semiology to then become semiotics, a much more fluid, less rigid application of Saussurian linguistics to social phenomena, which would dominate in the 1970s.

It was not just semiology and structuralism doing battle behind the scenes in the 1960s, but also semiology and sociology. Barthesian semiology was looking not just at clothing, but also food, suggesting that both of these objects displayed a central, fundamentally sociological, opposition in that they both 'classify their signifieds in virtue of the crucial cultural opposition between work and leisure' (Moriarty 1991: 80). For Moriarty this points to an overlap between semiology and sociology; but we can now see from the early preface to *The Fashion System* (chapter 7 here) that Barthes was keen to distinguish semiology sharply from sociology. Indeed, in the early period of the 1960s Barthes was moving swiftly away from sociology, despite references to Durkheimian method.[15] Carter (2003: 152–53) rightly underlines the sociological impulse to Barthes's writings on clothing history in the late 1950s, especially in the rejection of an evolutionary view of clothing forms. But Barthes now, in the early 1960s, wanted to leave behind the Gurvitchian sociological method he had defended in the early writings on clothing.

Rather than seeing social phenomena in relation to the *sum* of human individuals, Barthes now insisted that clothing showed 'the privileged example of a completely pure dialectic between the individual and society', as he put it in his 1962 piece on dandyism (chapter 6 here). This seemed to be at odds with Gurvitch's totalizing sociology, and is perhaps a central distinction between a sociology of clothing and a semiology of fashion.

So Nairn's strong reservations on Barthesian formalism in *The Fashion System* point then to a slippage operated by a tactical separation of semiology and sociology; it was a gap which allowed a structuralist optic, with the formalist and functionalist analyses that this entails, to dominate in *The Fashion System*. This growing formalism in Barthes's work on fashion explains perhaps why the 'Rhetorical' analysis, the ideological critique of fashion, is relegated to the end of the study, and has little of the social and political *engagement* evident in *Mythologies*.

However, as always in Barthes's work, discarded or relinquished positions always return at another, higher point in the spiral. Perhaps aware of the formalist, even empty, nature of his *magnum opus* on fashion – and influenced by the seismic radicalization of May 1968, which also exposed structuralism's technocratic tendencies – Barthes then moved in the post-1968 period towards much less formalist analyses of clothing.

But the main point that Barthes seemed to be making at the very end of the early preface to *The Fashion System* – which had distinguished semiology very clearly from sociology – was that semiology can (should) be used by sociology, by political critique and by ideological analysis. Here is the prelude to Barthes's (briefly held) view that semiology was a 'meta-language', the discipline that trumped all other disciplines because it recognized its and every other discipline's status as language. This was an idea to be heavily criticized by Henri Lefebvre (see Sheringham 2005: 305–6), and on which more in a moment.

Despite this (temporary) scientistic belief in the power of semiology it is important to stress the 'provisional' status of many of Barthes's theories and methods, especially in his use of semiology in relation to structuralism and to sociology. As with much of Barthes's work, his work on fashion emerged from teaching at the Ecole Pratique des Hautes Etudes in Paris, a fact reflected in the tentativeness with which he presents his scientific results. For example, though a

forerunner of *The Fashion System*,[16] "'Blue is in Fashion This Year'",
written in 1960, shows Barthes making surprisingly regular self-
reference – 'me', 'I', and not 'we' (something evident also in the
early preface to *The Fashion System*) – suggesting a rather cautious,
pre-scientific approach to a subject which was after all not what he
had looked at so far in his semiology, or in his analysis of clothing
across history.

The article's list of eighteen points suggests a rather modest and
clumsy approach, gesturing to the 'note' in the article's subtitle.
Barthes was working in highly uncharted waters here (not even
Kroeber managed this kind of detail); and though "'Blue is in
Fashion This Year'" clearly picked up on the concluding remarks
of his 1959 article 'Language and Clothing', Barthes now appears
slowly methodical in 1960, rather than glibly essayistic. This may
be the stirrings of his 'little scientific delirium', a rather fastidious
and calm search for a method and an object of study, culminating
in the (triumphant) thoroughness of *The Fashion System*; but it was
also the origins of what Jonathan Culler (1975: 35) calls Barthes's
methodological 'neglect' in *The Fashion System*.

Culler's critique of the method in *The Fashion System* seems to
revolve around Barthes's implicit decision to abandon sociology in
favour of a structuralist use of semiology. In its linguistic analysis
of what is in fashion, Barthes chose or neglected, argues Culler,
to suggest what the 'functional distinctions' were within any one
fashion utterance. As Culler puts it, 'It does not follow that each
descriptive term [in any fashion utterance] designates a feature
without which the garment would be unfashionable' (35). Similarly,
Culler regrets Barthes's restriction of his corpus to just one year. If
Barthes is interested in the fashion system in general, surely more
than one year should be analysed, argues Culler. Furthermore, the
oppositions in fashion that one finds between years – say, large one
year, or small another – cannot be analysed simply on distributional
grounds: they have a reality within fashion diachrony, suggests
Culler. Barthes's retort no doubt would be that to include any form
of diachrony in fashion motivations would be to reintroduce the
three notions of protection, ornamentation and modesty that he
had so readily rejected. In this sense, the method deployed in "'Blue
is in Fashion This Year'", and expanded and fine-tuned in *The*

*Fashion System*, follows on entirely from the delusion described in *Mythologies*: it is precisely how, by verbalizing, we convince ourselves of the fashionability of a form, or combination of clothing forms. Though language has become the basis of all human society across Barthes's work of the 1960s, he still maintains this interest in how language (including the verbalized image) is our link to the real. And it is here that Culler is less critical of *The Fashion System*. If Culler judges the vestimentary level of Barthes's work on the language of fashion as inadequate and confused, he is much more persuaded by the rhetorical level of analysis. The rhetorical analysis in *The Fashion System* suggests Culler (38–40) allows to us to see how paradoxical the language of fashion is actually, both empty and yet easy to fill with meaning, and in Culler's view this has an importance that goes beyond fashion and extends to the notion of 'realism' in literature, and thence society at large. 'Realism' – and by extension the 'real' – is what any one historical moment deems it to be.

Nevertheless, there is an order of tasks in *The Fashion System* that is fully prepared by the work leading up to it: Barthes wanted to isolate and analyse the system *before* looking at its rhetorical system. In dividing a semiology of fashion systems from a sociological interpretation of fashion forms – though the former 'opens doors' on to a sociology of fashion – Barthes seemed to be following Gilles-Gaston Granger's view that there is an ambiguity in using semiology to understand non-linguistic phenomena such as fashion.

Granger (1968: 133) was suggesting that there must be no confusion between a semiological analysis of a signifying system (i.e. fashion), with an interpretation of their 'meanings' within social praxis, that is with a '*philosophy* of advertising, political propaganda, cooking or clothes'. Granger took the example of election manifestos. In opposition to a sociological analysis of this material which looks at the potential electorate, at political phenomena which come before the manifesto, at previous campaigns, etc., Granger suggested that a semiological analysis would look instead at these manifestos as part of a system, showing how each one was a variant on various combinations, like the syntagms in a language. The aim was to show the connotative function of each 'text' and not necessarily an 'intentional' or 'conscious' mode. Nor should this be considered, Granger hinted, a 'comprehensive' analysis (as opposed to a 'causal' one), but as an attempt to lay bare the '*abstract* structuration' of the manifesto, and not a 'direct transposition of lived experience or of lived connections': semiology's originality then for Granger (and for Barthes) lay in its epistemological ability to 'structure the object', one which semiology borrows from language, a 'specifically human phenomenon' (134–35).

In the early preface to *The Fashion System*, Barthes showed himself to be equally dialectical in his view of totality. It is worth remembering that in 1963 'totality' did not yet hold any of the (Stalinized) 'totalitarian' connotations that critical Marxism and postmodernism have striven since to underline. Barthes uses totality (Carter 2003: 144, 147) but performs a critique of it at the same time, especially in relation to origins. The archetypes of fashion forms – military, sport, work, leisure (see chapter 18 of *The Fashion System*) – can 'explain' fashion forms, a diachronic approach can provide an 'etymology' of clothing styles, but they say very little about *how* fashion recombines them in any one fashion period. Combination and the language of presentation – the synchronic if you like – are as much a motor of form as 'origins'. In other words, Barthes seemed to be asking what was the relationship between totality (however provisional) and 'combination'? Surely totality was itself constantly changing, in flux. One example would be Barthes's four archetypes of clothing – military, sport, work and leisure – which see themselves augmented by events; hippies 'invent' another, fifth, archetype: the ethnic (or rustic/atavistic).

Indeed, Barthes was not at all insulated from a totalizing methodology. He referred regularly to the fact that men's fashion in the West is, fundamentally, archetypically, derivative of (English) Quaker fashion. Barthes is quite clearly adopting the spirit of Vladimir Propp's analysis of the folk tale (2000 [1928]) – in which, despite appearances, the forms (or the structures) that the world's folk tales took numbered barely more than seven in total – and then applying this to clothing in fashion.[17] Thus for Barthes, fashion and clothing are a 'poor' form of human culture, but which have three key 'enriching' possibilities: the combination of clothes items with its (almost) infinite number of possibilities; the detail – however small – which can radically inflect a style; and the language – written and/or visual representation – of the clothing item. Here semiology *is* the key method of inquiry, trumping all other disciplines. But as a dialectical form of enquiry – and this is a very dialectical time for Barthes and other critics using semiology – it cannot criticize itself from without: it is from within that it must provide its own auto-critique, a summary of its own shortcomings. It is here that semiology outstrips and inflects structuralism towards post-structuralism, towards changing itself into semiotics.

However, despite the very clear move away from sociology at the start of Barthes's 'high-structuralist' phase between 1963 and 1967, there is much that is still deeply sociological about his writing on clothing. Though *The Fashion System* is almost exclusively concerned with bourgeois (or perhaps, more likely, petty bourgeois) fashion forms and ideology, there are still hints of a wider, class-inflected consciousness at work. In addition to the sociological comments in *The Fashion System* on work and 'endimanchement' for the popular masses (see chapters 18.4 and 18.7), Barthes's 1961 piece on gem-stones and jewellery (chapter 5 here) suggested an important *sociological* point about access to fashion. The 'detail' seemed to be for Barthes an excellent example of how modern mass fashion was experiencing what we now tend to call a social 'levelling-up'. Just as the place where one shops for groceries in today's world is no longer a sign of one's social status, so access to fashion can be opened up by the addition of the smallest (and cheapest) of details which affect the overall fashion form adopted (Barthes's example being cheap, affordable jewellery). This 'democratization' of fashion is accompanied, he suggests, by a secularization of jewellery in which (and this clearly implies a socioeconomic dimension) cheaper materials such as wood, metal and glass can easily (and even preferably) stand in for their rare and priceless originals. Behind this attention to detail is Barthes's critique of the *simili*, what he had considered in *Mythologies* as petty bourgeois ideology's way of offering the poor and working population at least a *copy* of wealth and style and thereby a dream of social climbing. However, by 1962, this 'levelling-up' was not so much the *embourgeoisement* of the masses denounced in *Mythologies*, but a rather spurious guarantee of 'taste'.[18] Barthes did not explore the class connotations of this ideological function but it nevertheless has clear class connotations when considered alongside 'distinction' and the dandy's elitist desires.[19]

In fact, Barthes's constant *in*ability to get away from socioeconomic (or sociological) issues within fashion are clearly marked in his 1967 essay on Courrèges and Chanel, and even more so in his critique of hippy fashion (of which more below). Crucially, this linked back to the relationship between agency and institution: how much the self 'buys into' a system, and the rhetorical devices that the system uses to invite such a 'buying-in'.

## *History/Structure = Clothes/Fashion?*

Barthes, as always, seems a little lost between linguisticians who have very little to say for his semiology and historicists who berate his structuralism. And yet, the functionalism of his analyses has drawn applause. Luis Prieto considered Barthes's main contribution to semiology to be the 'function-sign', in which 'the utilitarian object is converted into a sign' (Moriarty 1991: 78), an example being the raincoat (Barthes 1968: 41–42), which keeps the rain off but which is also a sign of rain, to the extent that there can be 'raincoats' in fashion which do not even keep out the rain.[20] This was nevertheless an important development. Barthes's functionalism went back to his first article on clothing in 1957 (chapter 1 here). The example of the Roman *penula* that he gave in 'History and Sociology of Clothing' in 1957 was a clear break with the three-fold 'motivational' view of clothing. However, there does seem to be a further, or different, shift when he considered the raincoat in a similar way. For how would this functional analysis apply to the Roman *penula*? Would it be a sign of *Romanness*? Or would this interpretation be to place modern sign-systems anachronistically on to pre-modern phenomena? Must the semiology of fashion itself be synchronous in its insistence upon a synchrony of analysis? This is perhaps a good example of the history/structure dilemma: how do change and order relate to each other, across the human sciences and, as we shall see, the natural sciences?[21] On the level of Barthes's object – fashion – the dilemma is seen by him to be resolved (see *The Fashion System*, 20.12); but on the level of analysis, how history relates to structure is a complex question.

Given that Lévi-Strauss was acutely aware of the anti-historical claims made against structuralism (see Gaboriau in Lane 1970:

156–69) and that the Marxist anthropologist Maurice Godelier has tried to show that even Marx was a structuralist in his analysis of *Capital* (in Lane 1970: 340–58), the subtitle for this section of our essay is perhaps far too simplistic as a suggestion. As one critic has put it, 'structuralism is atemporal rather than strictly ahistorical' (Lane 1970: 17). This is important in our assessment of Barthesian fashion theory. Indeed, the history/structure tension was already being discussed by Barthes in the 1950s (see chapters 1 and 2 here, and Stafford 1998: chapter 2), with reverberations in the debate between *histoire événementielle* (the history of events) and *histoire de longue durée* which the *Annales* group, especially the work of Braudel, was instigating at the same time. Barthes was very aware in 1963 that the historical critique of structuralism came predominantly from Marxism (1972: 214) and during the 1960s other theorists such as Henri Lefebvre took up the history/structure debate in some detail.

In his 1966 critique of Lévi-Strauss, Lefebvre considered that the history/structure debate stretched back as far as the disagreement in Ancient Greece between Eleatists ('systemic' thinkers) and Heraclitans ('fluxists'), and was an important one for both Hegel and Marx. Lefebvre saw structuralism – or 'panstructuralism' in which he included Foucault's rejection of 'historicity' in favour of 'archaeology' – as a 'new Eleatism'.[22] Lefebvre's main argument was that structuralism discussed and used the notion of 'dimensions', but importantly not that of 'levels'; and, said Lefebvre (1975: 83), 'levels' only ever appeared once in Lévi-Strauss's work, in the latter's critique of the idea that synchrony and diachrony are separate (see chapter 7 here, note 18). But this was only part of Lefebvre's critique of structuralism.

The joust between Barthes and Lefebvre in the 1966 round-table discussion alongside Jean Duvignaud (chapter 8 here) represents a typical debate of the time on the semiological and structuralist methods then in vogue. Lefebvre is keen to assert a historical – some might say 'historicist' – dimension to the study of fashion forms, a view indicative of a wider debate on the Left at this time, in which 'Structure' and 'History' were seen as mutually exclusive. For a historical materialist such as Lefebvre, it was not so much 'system' that was anathema in the semiological and structuralist form of reasoning, but the evacuation of human agency, of materialist (or class) realities and of the historical and systemic provenance of state and class power. Furthermore, despite recent attempts to see demystification as common interests in Barthes's and Lefebvre's earlier work (Kelly 2000), Lefebvre is a general critic of structuralism, and as we can see in the 1966 round-table discussion, there are flashes in the argument of what Carter calls the 'endogeny' debate, the extent to which history interferes with changes in fashion forms (2003: 160–61), to which we will return in a moment. Lefebvre comes to see structuralism in particular as a technocratic mode of analysis mobilized by capitalism (and a fast-expanding one in 1960s France) to reorganize French industry. It is no surprise then that Lefebvre becomes a key player in the May 1968 rejection of technocracy, whilst Barthes is mildly taunted by the Paris students in revolt for being a 'Structure' that does not 'take to the streets' (Calvet 1994: chapter 8).

So Lefebvre criticized structuralism at its macro, sociopolitical level and he also looked critically at its micro, semiological levels. Long before May 1968, Lefebvre's work on language had been quick to pick up on Barthes's work on semiology and his attempt to apply language to clothing. Even though Lefebvre has time for Barthes's work – Barthes is the only structuralist that he engages with, as Elden points out – he regretted that Barthes 'dismisses sociology on behalf of semiology' (quoted in Elden 2003: 113). The debate hinges on whether Barthes accepts that, like language, clothing has a 'double articulation': for, argues Lefebvre, 'there are elementary items of clothing (underwear, trousers or skirt, jacket or shirt, etc. perhaps liable to be classified by pertinent aspects, like phonemes would be) and meaningful ensembles (perhaps equivalent to morphemes)' (64). Lefebvre's point is that in considering clothing as 'syntactic' rather than 'lexical', Barthes was avoiding the question of double articulation. Indeed, in the early preface to *The Fashion System* (chapter 7 here), Barthes does not take a position on double articulation; nor does he seem to in *Elements of Semiology*, merely describing it in neutral terms. For Lefebvre, the double articulation is the main element which divides the scientific linguistic community (Martinet, Mounin), from the semiological tendency involving a more artistic and literary view of language in which he includes Barthes, Jakobson, but also Trubetskoy and Lévi-Strauss, and for whom the science of language is a meta-language.[23] In other words, for Lefebvre, in not insisting upon a double articulation in language – in which language is both morphological and phonological, though these levels are distinctly separate – Barthes (et al.) cannot claim a scientific rigour. This is despite the fact that, later on, Lefebvre seems to side with Barthes against Martinet in seeing the most powerful form of human acts of communication as semiological, rather than simply linguistic as the pure linguisticians such as Martinet would have it (316). It is clear, then, that at a micro semiological level, as well as at a macro political one, the relationship of history to structure is a complex one and not easily resolved.

The discussion as to the relationship between history and structure raises the question of analogy and its appropriateness. Is it analogical (even homological) to use linguistics (in Barthes's case) to explain fashion? I have argued elsewhere that Barthes was suspicious of analogy, especially in relation to historiography, in its tendency to ignore specificity (Stafford 1998: chapter 2). But is applying linguistics to fashion a form of analogy?[24] Moriarty points out (1991: 76) that in his work on food, clothes and shelter, Barthes was aware that the *langue/parole* relationship was not identical: in fashion for example, individuals cannot act back on the system in the same way that they can in language as it is spoken. It is clear that, though Barthes is very wary of linking clothing form *directly* to history – and explicitly so at regular moments in his work on fashion, making sharp differences with Lefebvre in the round-table discussion in this book – he nevertheless mobilizes historical society and societies to explain the function of various substances and phenomena in clothing. For example, his is a deeply historicist explanation of the disappearance of dandyism. Fashion, he argues, 'killed off' this distinctly nineteenth-century phenomenon when the manufactured uniformity of type allowed for the infinite variety of detail. Similarly, gemstones, once part of prehistoric society, became jewellery in modern society. With regard to historical influence, the question then becomes, what constitutes 'direct' and 'indirect'? Without the caveats of a Kroeber, there is a danger, especially with regard to a radical decade such as the 1960s, that we infer directly from history the forms that fashion takes. This is not to say that Barthes dismisses history as an important category – and some of his comments on historical influence on clothing forms come surprisingly close to some of those by James Laver (see Carter 2003: 127); but his is a structural use of history, not a 'Zeitgeist' one. And though sensitive to Flügel's work, which tries to place historically defined social mores on to fashion changes (Carter 113), Barthes is distinctly more Kroeberian in his historical formalism.[25] So, whilst bearing in mind this limit placed on 'Zeitgeist' theory, an overview of the distinctly literary dimension to Barthes's fashion theory in the 1960s may be useful to determine questions of analogy and fashion form.

## *The 1960s, From Clothes to Fashion; or: Fashion as Literature*

Fashion does not interest me. I don't know what fashion is; what interests me is style: they are two completely different things. Fashion is something superficial, a regular change, dependent on tastes, moods, which has nothing to do with real style. Style is the true result that emerges from our times.

*André Courrèges (in Lemoine-Luccioni 1983)*

Couture is for grannies.

*Brigitte Bardot (in Lobenthal 1990)*

It was perhaps typical of the 1960s that it brought together a method of fashion analysis based on the 'shifter' in language that Barthes initiated, alongside the (now) classic 1960s fashionable dress called the shift.[26] The 1960s were after all a decade of revolution in social and political realities as well as in fashion. It was also the period when Paris lost its worldwide fashion status as the ready-to-wear culture began to challenge the elitism of haute couture (Lobenthal 1990: 41). Whereas early 1950s fashion in France was estimated to be 85 per cent handmade, by 1966 more than two-thirds was factory-made.[27] As Eric Hobsbawm has recently suggested (2002: 261), it was not only the collapse in 1965 in the number training to be priests that set the 1960s in France alight; it may also have been the moment when the French clothing industry produced more trousers than skirts. With what Hobsbawm ironically calls the 'forward march of jeans' as the 'significant index of the history of the second half of the twentieth century', Dior's 1947 New Look was now up for challenge and parody. So alongside André Courrèges, the houses of Ungaro, Cardin, Estérel, Rabanne and Saint Laurent all began to undermine the elitism of an outfit by Dior or Chanel. As Courrèges himself put it, 'I'm the Ferrari, Chanel the old Rolls, still in working order but inert' (cited in Madsen 1990: 300).[28] And in the 1960s Chanel was simply 'subtly reworking the same styles' (de la Haye/ Tobin 1994: 105), and Courrèges's very mode of presentation, let alone his outfits, was 'diametrically opposed to the couture status quo' (Lobenthal 1990: 50).

Barthes seemed to side with the modern designers such as Courrèges in his 1967 *Marie Claire* article on the 'Chanel versus Courrèges' duel and was the first to suggest, according to Vincent-Ricard (1987: 80), that 1960s youth 'no longer needs to be either vulgar or distinguished, it simply is'. Barthes is even credited with helping Courrèges's sales; Valérie Guillaume (1998: 4) wonders if Barthes's piece in *Marie Claire* did not show those women fond of Chanel's timeless chic how to wear Courrèges's 'new' look. However, it is the fundamentally literary way in which Barthes inserted himself into the fashion debates of the 1960s that was perhaps his key success.

Michel Butor (1974: 384) suggests that the only reason Barthes looked at the written language of women's fashion was that women's language was taboo for men, which Barthes could then break with his pseudo-scientific language of semiology. In fact, Butor concluded, the way for *The Fashion System* to ward off any scientific criticism of its method was to make itself into a book of literature (385).[29] The distinctly literary take is unmistakeable in Barthes's analyses of fashion forms. Indeed, there was in Barthes's thought on clothing, as we saw, a clear move towards its 'literarization', in both senses of the word. Across the period covered in this anthology, it is clearly language which becomes his dominant mode of enquiry and explanation. But also, Barthes seems to allow Fashion and Literature to dovetail in a number of key ways.

In 1959 (see chapter 2 here) Barthes possibly realized that his project on the history of clothing forms was far too large and perhaps ultimately futile (to use one of his regular expressions in relation to clothing histories), leading him to devise, instead, a synchronic study of fashion. However, it could also lead us to conclude that the move towards a literarization of fashion was dependent on the semiological turn that Barthes's thought had taken since 1956. Furthermore, this literarization of sociological thought would necessarily draw on literature, the literary, because the writing alongside images of fashionable outfits in fashion magazines used language in a rhetorical style which then chimed with the consumer's 'taste'. Barthes makes this point clearly in '"Blue is in Fashion This Year"', calling this rhetorical writing an 'écriture', albeit a 'poor literature'.

Though this is a linguistic (rather than strictly literary) understanding, in an interview the following year in 1961, he famously compared literature and fashion (1972: 152), describing both as 'homeostatic systems', their function being 'not to communicate ... but only to create a functioning equilibrium'; they signify 'nothing', he suggested, and 'their essence is in the process of signification, not in what they signify'.

As early as 1959, Barthes was talking about clothes as a '*text without end*' (see chapter 2 here). Furthermore, the mid-1960s was a moment when more modernist literary values could be part of a challenge to the growing consumerist culture of de Gaulle's technocratic France. Georges Perec's 1965 novel *Les Choses*, subtitled a 'history of the 1960s', is an anti-materialist take on fashion, with the main characters, Jérome and Sylvie, able to understand only the language of labels and materials. It was an early example of young people becoming aware and radicalized by society's tendency to encourage us, in Erich Fromm's words, 'to have rather than to be'. Literature, modern literary criticism, the literary, could act as a corrosive, destabilizing, even 'terroristic (Sheringham 2005: 305), element in the seemingly harmonious world of shopping in Monoprix. At the centre of a quarrel with arch-conservative and Sorbonne Racine specialist, Raymond Picard, over traditional literary criticism and its values, Barthes was well qualified for this role. One glance at his 1967 piece on Chanel and Courrèges – especially the opening paragraph – shows not only where Barthes stood whilst watching the duel, but how much literature, the literary, was his guiding light, as Chanel is shown by Barthes to be rather traditional and patrician in her deployment of literary culture.[30]

Here Barthes's work on literature and fashion began to dovetail. His view of what he had done in *S/Z*, his reading and rewriting of Balzac's *Sarrasine* in 1968 and 1969, could easily be applied (if retrospectively) back to his work on fashion: 'I have changed the level of perception of the object' he commented to Stephen Heath in 1971 (1985b: 135), 'and in so doing I have changed the object'. Semiology and structuralism had therefore brought about a change in the act of the critic, what Barthes calls elsewhere 'parametrism' (1972 [1964]: 275): 'in the order of perception, if you change the level of perception, you end up changing the object' (1985b: 135).[31]

Already in a 1967 interview (1994: 458), again speaking of literary study in a way that could be applied to his analysis of fashion, Barthes opined: 'It is linguistics that has allowed us to avoid the impasse which sociologism and historicism brings us to, and which consists of excessively reducing history to the history of referents', thereby ignoring, he added (in deference to Braudel's multiple dimensions of history) the 'plural' aspect of historical moments. It was the signifier – not the possible signifieds that it generated – that needed to be privileged in the new post-1968 world. Indeed, written in the wake of May 1968, the opening paragraphs of *S/Z* are exemplary in showing how the human sciences, writing, the literary, now needed to escape the overarching, all-defining, totalizing systems of structuralism, to (re)discover both the singular and its infinite possibilities of combination.[32] It is for this reason, in part, that we decided to include in this anthology the 'Showing How Rhetoric Works' article (which appeared in *Change* in 1969), even though it is clear that this piece is not 'original', rather a collection of (slightly edited) fragments from *The Fashion System* which had appeared two years before. For what is interesting about these collected fragments from *The Fashion System* is precisely their own 'recombination' (or *combinatoire*): whether it was Barthes himself or the editors of this special number of the journal on fashion who selected choice moments of his magisterial analysis of the rhetoric of the fashion system, the selection made is indicative of the journal's radical take on fashion, a radical moment in fashion theory to which we will return in a moment.

Seeing Literature in Fashion, or Fashion as Literature, was an important element of Barthesian fashion theory, modelling the way in which it looked at the influence or otherwise of history on form. To literarize 'fashion', to equate the world of fashion with that of literature was to formalize clothing and its attendant myths and means of communication in order to dismantle the model. But literarization ran the risk of being formalist and thereby of losing its political charge and its ideological critique.

It is not a coincidence that a (short) answer to what constitutes 'direct' and 'indirect' with regard to historical influence on fashion form comes at the start of Barthes's writing on Racine in 1960, at the very moment when the 'language of fashion' was foremost in his mind: 'Forms resist, or worse still, they do not change at the same rate' (1992 [1963]: 154). Here is the paradox in Barthes's theory then, something that remains constant throughout his critique of histories of fashion: that history and form are not at all directly linked – and a study such as that by van Thienen (1961), which takes clothing as a direct peel-off from historical events, would be anathema to a Barthes trying to explain clothing forms internally. But then again, literature is, as we have seen, clearly an analogical horizon for Barthes working on fashion.[33] So form (and the changes in form) cannot simply be inferred by historical changes; and yet theories on how form relates to history can be applied across phenomena (here, from fashion to literature, and then back): Barthes's theory of form therefore *needs* a level of analogy in which history plays a paradoxical role. This has important consequences for the question of form, interpretation and politics (and their very interrelation) in Barthes's fashion theory. We are now in a position to come to some tentative conclusions on the radical-interpretative and scientific-formalist tensions in Barthes's writing on fashion.

## Conclusion: Back to Interpretation?

One should either be a work of art, or wear a work of art.

*Oscar Wilde*

Fashion is nothing but what one says it is.

*Roland Barthes (1972 [1961])*

It is not easy to say whether clothes really *are* part of human primal character but they are certainly 'semantic engines' (to quote Daniel Dennett). And perhaps one of Barthes's enduring (and distinctly humanist) notions within fashion theory is the idea that as consumers we *verbalize*, constantly and continually, our relationship to clothing forms. However, this is only a *formal* explanation of fashion and clothing. What about its content? That 'fashion is structured on the level of its history', may be incontestable in Barthes's work; but, he also argued, in the appendix on Kroeber in *The Fashion System* that 'It is destructured on the only level that we see of it: present-dayness' (1985a: 299, translation modified). Indeed, much as Barthes claimed to be a 'formalist', to be highly wary if not sceptical of attempts to link form to history, and to link form to ideological content, nevertheless his reading of hippies in 1969 (chapter 12 here) is precisely that. Having suggested in 1966 that it was wrong to infer a feminization of young men from the move to long hair influenced by the Beatles – there is no form which is inherently feminine, he insists, in the round-table discussion (chapter 8 here) – his 1969 view of hippies does involve a structural interpretation of the hippies' social revolt via clothing styles.

It is worth pointing out that Barthes's critique of hippy clothing and style, 'A Case of Cultural Criticism' (chapter 12 here), was published in a section of the *Communications* special number in 1969 on 'Cultural Politics' called 'The Situation and the Political Challenge made by Cultural Action'; and Barthes's conclusion – that the hippy is an 'inverted bourgeois' – reflected the journal's radical critique of 'recuperation' following the May 1968 events. Though his is a content-based description – one which his earlier fashion work seemed to want to avoid – it is also a highly political one. The lifestyle politics of the hippy – the form of the hippy's politics if you like, and here Barthes may be seen to be true to his formalist leanings – does not manage to break with the established, dominant ideology underpinning normal social and cultural praxis. A similar point could be made about his view that Chanel's invention of a woman's suit goes back to a period of history when a minority of women were beginning to go out to work (see chapter 11 here). However, beneath the skilful essayism of the final paragraph of this essay in *Marie Claire* – in which Barthes neatly steps out of, or offers us the chance to step outside, fashion – there is evidence perhaps of a tiredness with fashion as an object of semiological study; and thus 'interpretation' – rather than a systematic treatment of fashion language – can be seen to make a (brief) return in his work.[34] It is May 1968 which acts as the main catalyst towards this return to interpretation.

We need only look at the difference in tone between Barthes's only piece on fashion written after May 1968 (excepting the extracts from *The Fashion System* appearing in *Change*) and what has gone before it. Indeed, the radical Nietzschean negativity evident in 'A Case of Cultural Criticism' was redolent of a general political climate on the Left at the time.[35] This is despite the fact that Barthes's critique of hippies has itself been criticized for his own 'orientalist', stereotyping tendencies. Diana Knight (1997: 129ff, 176) points out that the critique of an 'ideologically dubious parody of Moroccan poverty', in which Barthes contrasts the Western hippy with the poor Moroccan peasants' true poverty, may be weakened by Barthes's own account of his search for a blue djellaba in *Incidents* (written in Morocco at the same time as the article on hippy fashion). However, in my view, his critique of hippies' economically poor *chic* appears much less ironic when we consider other thoughts on poverty in Morocco. In 'Brecht and Discourse: a Contribution to the Study of Discursivity' in 1975 (Barthes 1986: 212–22), in the section called 'The Sign' (219–21), Barthes's semiological and Brechtian analysis of the policeman's shoes (perfectly shined and in immaculate condition) contrasts them with those worn by the destitute boy who is being hassled off the beach by the policeman. It is the boy's shoddy shoes which are an indelible social marker, he argues with deep pathos, revealing a Barthes acutely aware of the reality behind the 'signs' of socioeconomic alienation.

But Barthes's criticism of hippy fashion is also not just a gay writer suspicious of young men in drag-like clothes, but primarily someone unable to see social change coming from the hippies (signalled here in his reflections on real poverty, or destitution). And implicitly Barthes seems to see the (hippy) Bohemian as the 'structural opposite' of the Dandy, echoing Georg Simmel's critique of the Bohemian (see Carter 2003: 74). For Barthes is acutely sensitive to the radical post-1968 idea of 'recuperation', to the possibility that hippy fashion is merely another example of what George Melly called 'revolt into style' (1970).[36] Here the special number of *Change*, in which the fragments from *The Fashion System* were published in 1969, became part of the radical critique of post-1968 French culture as one of 'recuperation'. Referring to a piece by Marx from an unpublished section of *Capital* that had (apparently) been first published in *Change* a year before (no. 2, 1968), this special number in 1969, called 'Fashion – invention', included this quote from the German revolutionary: 'Fashionable subversion is a conservative subversion – an *upside-down* staging – which the effect of development and discovery ironically engenders and then *destroys*'.[37] This (little-known) quote from Marx was indicative of the radical tone that *Change* and other journals were taking in the aftermath of May 1968.[38] In the 1971 interview with Stephen Heath, Barthes therefore argued the following with regard to semiology and its success in education: 'Once an institution becomes involved, one can say that there is recuperation' (1985b: 130), and he blamed the scientific version of semiology for this. However, as always with Barthes, things are never straightforward. Just as 'interpretation' seemed to return to his analysis of fashion forms in the post-1968 period, his 1971 comments on fashion designers now appeared far from critical.

Discussing the stylish alphabet designed by Erté and reminding the reader that the Italian artist was originally a fashion designer, Barthes asked rhetorically: 'Are not couturiers the poets who, from year to year, from strophe to strophe, write the anthem of the feminine body?' (1986: 113). For like poetry or literature, a fashion form cannot be 'explained': 'Each time Fashion notably changes (for instance, shifting from long to short), we find reporters eagerly questioning the psychologists and sociologists to discover what new Woman will be generated by the miniskirt or the sack. A waste of time as it turns out: no one can answer'. For Barthes now in 1971, acutely aware (as we saw above) of the 'recuperation' operated by post-1968 cultural systems, 'No discourse can be based on Fashion, once it is taken as the symbolic *expression* of the body'. Therefore, in that fashion cannot 'traverse, develop, describe its symbolic capacity', it 'seeks clarity, not pleasure'; it is 'not obsessed by the body' but by 'the Letter, the body's inscription in a systematic space of signs', that is 'the general sign-system which makes our world intelligible to us, i.e. liveable' (114–15). So again, Barthes seemed to be swinging back to a *non-*interpretative fashion theory. It was also, as he acknowledged, a challenge to a certain orthodoxy set up by Hegel (which Barthes had happily cited in *The Fashion System*, chapter 18.11), and a discussion of which we must now engage in for the conclusion of this Afterword.

Barthes articulates his critique of Hegel by way of the silhouette in Erté's drawings of women in his alphabet: 'Hegel has noted that the garment is responsible for the transition from the sensuous (the body) to the signifier; the Ertéan silhouette (infinitely more thought out than the fashion mannequin) performs the contrary movement (which is more rare): it makes the garment sensuous and the body into the signifier; the body is there (signed by the silhouette) in order for the garment to exist; it is not possible to conceive a garment without the body...' Thus, in a complete reversal of our 'modesty' view of clothing, fashion does not exist, Barthes seemed to be suggesting, in order to cover the body; rather it is the body which is the *support* for the garment. This is fine as far as a conception of clothes' relationship to the body goes, but Barthes was maybe being a little unfair on Hegel; and this has a bearing on our assessment of Barthesian fashion theory. For, what Barthes does *not* say about Hegel's account of clothes is that Hegel, though writing as early as the 1820s (see 1975: 742–50, esp. 746–48), was deeply conscious of 'modern' clothing and fashion, particularly in its opposition to the ancient Greek conception of clothes and specifically to the way in which classical sculpture represented this conception. What is interesting in looking back at Hegel after reading Barthes is just how much of Hegelian thought returns, in spiral, in Barthes's fashion theory. Indeed, it is difficult not to see the reasons for Hegel's dismissal of modern clothing as parallel, if not central, to Barthes's own inversion as outlined in his discussion of Erté.

'Ideal art', as Hegel calls it, like clothing, 'conceals the super-
fluity of the organs which are necessary, it is true for the body's
self-preservation, for digestion etc., but for the expression of the
spirit, otherwise superfluous' (745). The key expression here, and
distinctly Hegelian, is 'expression of the spirit'. For what Hegel seems
to be saying is that nudity is a direct contrast to the expression of the
'spirit' in clothes. And so, just as Barthes tries to invert the relationship
between clothes and body, between signified and signifier, to arrive
at a more modern – dare I say 'symbolist' – understanding of clothing forms and fashion statements, so precisely does Hegel with
nudity. Rather than seeing nudity in classical Greek sculpture from
the 'modesty' point of view, Hegel sees nudity itself as a signifier
of strength, of spiritual beauty, in both its naivety and ingenuity.[39]
In fact the whole point of Hegel's discussion – and this fits with
Barthes's own work on the 'realism' of representation in sculpture
in his reading of Balzac's short story *Sarrasine* – is that modern
clothing may *seem* to be 'most advantageous' in the way that 'closely
fitting clothes' do very little to conceal the shape of the limbs or the
posture of the human being, and 'are the least hindrance because
they make visible the whole form of the limbs as well as Man's walk
and his gestures' (746). But this 'advantage' is shallow and empty
for Hegel: 'What we really see in [modern clothing, as represented
in modern statues and pictures] ... is not the fine, free, and living
contours of the body in their delicate and flowing development but
stretched-out sacks with stiff folds' (746). Ancient Greek clothing as
displayed in the art of antiquity, by contrast, argues Hegel, 'is a more
or less explicitly formless surface..., [it] remains plastic and simply
hangs down freely in accordance with its own immanent weight'.
'What constitutes the ideal in clothing' suggests Hegel then, 'is the
determining principle displayed when the outer wholly and entirely
subserves the changeable expression of spirit appearing in the body'
(164). In other (Barthesian) words, the body in Hegelian thought
ought to have a formless clothing covering it, a covering in which
the body is the signifier and the latter 'adapted to precisely [the]
pose or movement momentarily only' of the body wearing it. This
is a dialectical (rather than strictly semiological) understanding of
clothing as formless, infinitely changeable in line with the flux of
the shape of the body as signifier. Indeed, Hegel's reasoning may be
far different from Barthes's – 'Such clothing is in fact just a covering

and a veil which throughout lacks any form of its own, but, in the organic formation of the limbs which it follows in general, precisely conceals what is visibly beautiful, namely their living swelling and curving, and substitutes for them the visible appearance of a material mechanically fashioned'; but Barthes's suggestion that couturiers should be seen as 'poets' echoes perfectly the 'artistic' that Hegel is looking for in clothing, albeit in its sculptural representation. Furthermore, Barthes's claim that 'It is not possible to conceive a garment without the body' is precisely what Hegel seems to be saying in seeing the ideal clothing as 'formless'. In other words, clothing for Hegel – and it seems also for Barthes (by 1971 at least) – should *show* (or signify) the body in its all its sensuousness, a sensuousness which is signified by the very clothes worn. Unless we fall back on to nudity and its beauty as a desired form, it is the *literal* nature of clothing that unites Barthes and Hegel in their conception of appropriate clothing forms (Hegel's 'artistic' clothes would be those worn by ancient Greeks, but Barthes does not pronounce on any preferred forms). 'Our manner of dress, as outer covering', concludes Hegel, 'is insufficiently marked out by our inner life to appear conversely as shaped from within' (166). The key point then is that Hegelian clothing theory anticipates – though, in good deconstructive fashion, it is only by reading Barthes's theories on the matter that we can see this – the modern, anti-psychological and deeply functionalist view of clothes often adopted by Barthes's fashion theory. This view inverts the body – sensuous/clothes – signifier (or 'scientific') opposition, to produce the clothes – sensuous/body – signifier (or 'poetic') attitude to clothing form and its function. Barthes's formalism – tinged inevitably, if parsimoniously, by an ideological critique – is perhaps more indebted to Hegelian formalism than we might have expected.

Interestingly, in one of his last comments on fashion – in a 1978 interview on the body, 'Encore le corps' – Barthes now seemed happy to accept Hegel's original assertion: 'Clothing is the moment when the sensuous becomes signifier, i.e. when clothing is that through which the human body becomes signifier and thus a bearer of signs, of its own signs even' (Barthes 1995: 912–18).[40] So what seems to be happening in his ongoing thoughts on the Hegelian view of clothes, is that, with different objects coming into Barthes's sights (fashion, Erté's silhouetted alphabets, and then the body), he adopts and reshapes Hegel's thoughts on clothing forms. It is perhaps glib then to see the (apparent) heterogeneity of clothing forms that Barthes sees in 1978, as La Croix does (1987: 75), as a sign of 'postmodernity': for Barthes is, it would seem, merely 'bending the stick' towards heterogeneity as he is (here) discussing the body (not fashion as such) or rather fashion's effect on the body; and were Barthes to discuss fashion per se in 1978, doubtless he would be less convinced of this heterogeneity on a social and systematic scale. So, given Jobling's critique of Barthes's work on fashion as logocentrically *anti*-postmodern (see note 14 here) and de la Croix's view of Barthes as postmodern, we are merely reminded of how irrelevant 'postmodern' theory is to understanding Barthes's work on fashion: the engagement with Hegel clearly points to Barthes's attempts to found a modern if not modernist conception of clothing.

However, with cultural recuperation seemingly unstoppable in 1970s France, Barthes appears, as we saw above, less than critical in his account of couturiers and of the fashion political economy in general. Indeed, Fortassier argues (1988: 215) that Barthes is one of the modern sociologists of fashion who are happy to 'excuse' the fashion-conscious woman who changes her wardrobe every season, by considering this 'modern form of waste' as a part of the ostentatious and ancient form of human 'potlatch', in which appearance was considered magical, and whose contemporary counterpart is found (in Barthes's words) in the 'heavy wearing-effect of time'. Fortassier (216) points out that for the semiologist – and Barthes is implicitly included in this – fashion is nothing 'but a system of empty signs'; 'fashion clothing signifies incessantly, but it signifies nothing' and thus fashion is like literature when 'it refuses functionality'. Fashion may be literary in the way that it quotes from the history of language utterances and clichés, but it is when fashion communicates (Mallarmé's) nothingness that it comes closest to the literary, argues Fortassier. She is following the 'late' Barthes for whom the very emptiness of Haiku poetry is a Zen-like 'degree zero' of meaning, where the 'babble' of language and meaning is momentarily (and perhaps rather utopianly) suspended, a babble which, if current fashion shows are anything to go by (Mullan 2002), is seemingly getting worse.

The pleasure and promotion of the signifier in the early 1970s was trademark Barthesian 'textuality' and it culminated, in fashion terms, with the view that Erté's feminized alphabet reverses the usual conception of the body and clothing within appearance, to suggest that the female fashion model prolongs the fashion item through her body, and not (as we might expect) the other way round. This could be seen as a formalist game of inverting functions, uses and bodily aesthetics, or alternatively as a deconstructive, terroristic attack on fixed ideas of form and content, on the latent/manifest relationship, which equalizes (or 'de-hierarchizes') the function and form of the human body in relation to clothing, a tactic that is classic post-1968 avant-garde essayism. Perhaps Barthes is also suggesting that it is facile, false to find or even look for the personality behind or in clothing. This is not simply because the self/apparel relationship is a deeply complex one, but also because the self itself is a complex one, locked in a dialectic of hiding and showing for which clothing is ultimately a poor and limited communicator. And it may be that Barthes too is a victim of fashion. Godfrey (1982: 32) argues that the death of the dandy has been prematurely announced, seeing the dandy as essentially an ironic figure, both inside and outside society: we might suggest then that Barthes himself could wear the 'dandy' label without too much difficulty, and this certainly in terms of his own literary or intellectual 'fashionability'.

But 'newness' theory, as deployed by Lipovetsky (1994), cannot be applied to all of Barthes's work and then be allowed to expel 'distinction' (or class-based, historical theories) on fashion. It is too simplistic perhaps to see Barthes's structuralism as one which 'evacuates' the human subject: on the contrary, the manner in which the signifier–signified link is conceived by Barthes implies a much more voluntaristic (not passive) dimension to signification and to those values placed on clothing forms (Carter 2003: 155–56). This essay has shown, I hope, that these two conceptions of fashion – as 'constraint' and as 'appropriation' – do not (necessarily) stand in opposition to each other, as Stern (2004: 2) seems to imply, but sit, as they do in Barthes's own work, in a tension.

Is it too 'liberal' then to allow this tension to be a signifier of a much wider set of problems – encapsulated in the various contradictions that we have discussed here? Is this tension tantamount to seeing fashion as a form of (paradoxically) *mass* avant-garde cultural praxis? Then again, it is all very well to pronounce this oxymoron, indicative of a highly innovative creativity by the masses within the social 'institution' of fashion forms; but what about the mathematical reality of this, the mass ideology, the dialectically multipliable 'double-consciousness' of the individual? In other words, have we *really* got past the radical Marxian idea which sees advertising – fashion being one amongst many of its forms – as alienated *and* alienating? Is commodity fetishism, as postmodern theory would have it (Kohan 2005), now *really* an irrelevant category in contemporary fashion theory? It is his cultural formalism – the ability to sit 'inside' people's minds as they commune with the garment, and at the same time the ability to stand outside and point to fashion's nakedness before human justice and equality – that makes Barthes, ultimately, into a *conciliatory* theorist, dialectically arbitrating (or vacillating) between opposing camps, but never abandoning either position definitively: Barthes, particoloured like the jester of the Middle Ages, both fool and wise man, both inside and outside of fashion, the dandy of modern ideas.

## Notes

1. Exceptions to this (other than Carter 2003) include Culler 1975, Lavers 1982, Moriarty 1991 and Sheringham 2005, which we will discuss during this essay.

2. Sheringham even includes Walter Benjamin and Georg Simmel in this 'positive' camp (2005: 306–12).

3. Indeed, up until recently, as Diana de Marly points out (1986), working dress has 'seldom received the attention it deserves in histories of costume, which continues to concentrate on fashion for the privileged few' (dust cover).

4. See Greimas, *La mode en 1830. Essai de description du vocabulaire vestimentaire d'après les journaux de mode de l'époque,* and *Quelques reflets de la vie sociale en 1830 dans le vocabulaire des journaux de mode de l'époque,* thesis and second thesis (1948) for a 'doctorat-ès-lettres' at the Faculté des Lettres de l'Université de Paris. These theses have recently been republished (Greimas 2000).

5. 'L'actualité du saussurisme', *Le Français Moderne* 24 (1956), 191–203 (republished in Greimas 2000 : 371–82). Unfortunately none of the early Greimas work has been translated, only those writings from 1962 onwards that cover his work on narrative structures are available in English; see Greimas, *On Meaning. Selected Writings on Semiotic Theory*, trans. Paul Perron and Frank Collins, London, Frances Pinter, 1987.

6. As Greimas himself had done, Barthes's *Mythologies* repeated the misrecognition of Hjelmslev's 'meta-language' as the language of connotation, (see Arrivé in Greimas 2000: xix). Arrivé underlines how much Greimas's two theses needed to use Saussure's theories much earlier in his doctoral work (xiii); and yet, Greimas's decision to work on the year 1829–1830 made his analysis deeply synchronic, and, though clearly not about development, it clearly invites a historical reading if one then looks at the same vocabulary before and after the period studied.

7. However, the clearest and most specific influence from Greimas is the choice and method of clothes and fashion (not to mention the 1830 date for Balzac's *Sarrasine*), for it is the language of 1830 (and the use of Vladimir Propp's theories which are central to Greimas's work in the 1960s) that permeates Barthes's reading of Balzac's gothic story in *S/Z*.

8. Indeed, it might not be too far-fetched to consider Barthes's work on fashion as a continuation of Kroeber's search for a formal law of fashion forms, especially given that Kroeber's own time-line for fashion cycles (anywhere from 75 to 125 years) goes beyond the lifespan of any one human individual. And here Barthes's fascination with Michelet's historiography was a fundamental influence – how to stand within, and simultaneously outside, history.

9. There is a debt also, as I have suggested elsewhere (Stafford 1998: 26–28), to Trotsky's 'long' view of the rise of capitalism.

10. Perrot writes: 'Yet though we have many histories of dress, it is difficult to find systematic connections between dress styles and the chronology of politics. Changes of regime, ideological upheavals, and transformations in mores sometimes superficially influence the pace and content of fashion, but these variations take place within slow oscillations', and, he adds, 'analogous to the deeper tendencies that economists perceive beneath rapid day-to-day price

movements. The regular evolution of these tendencies is rarely disturbed by historical events. In fact, like economic history, cultural history marches to a different drummer' (31).

11. The influence of 'detail' in the theatre is central to Barthes's subsequent work on fashion; see for example the use of detail in his 1960 preface to Roger Pic's photographs of the Berliner Ensemble (Barthes 1993a: 893–94), in which Barthes suggests that the tiniest clothing detail – a half-opened neck of a shirt for example – becomes a cipher of the human body's 'vulnerability', and therefore of humanity's 'tenderness' central to Brechtian theatre.

12. See 'The Illuminated Body' section and the 'drag' example in *Sade, Fourier, Loyola* (1977a: 128).

13. And Barthes's sensitivity to fashion photography, and to what it does and does not do, is evident as early as 1959 (see chapter 2 here, note 15).

14. Jobling (1999) attempts to recontextualize and criticize what he calls Barthes's 'logocentric anti-postmodern' concentration on written fashion. By contrast, Jobling aims to show a 'complementarity' between written and visual (re)presentation of fashion in the photograph, by suggesting that a decoding reading of both fashion photograph and caption must be operated 'in tandem' (91), neither privileging nor relegating either text or image. Thus, rather glibly, he describes Barthes's view of the writing of the photograph as sitting somewhere in between 'anchorage and relay', in which the former suggests a 'harmonious narrative structure' and the latter a 'conflictual tension'. But Jobling offers no thoughts on the deeply complex interaction of image/text that Barthes analyses in 'The Photographic Message'. Firstly, it is worth underlining that, given Barthes's fascination with the interface of word and image (especially photographs), it seems odd to take Barthes's division of word from image in fashion at face value (as Jobling does, 72–74), or as set in stone. Surely the division is a methodological and procedural one; and maybe Barthes's main point is to underline not so much the paucity of fashion (photography) as a system (though, undoubtedly, he *is* suggesting this), but of its written form; for Barthes concedes that the image 'freezes an endless number of possibilities [whereas] words determine a single certainty' (Barthes 1985a: 13, 14, 119). This comment implies that the

writing of photography can be so much richer than that found in the captioning or 'ekphrasis' (i.e. interpretation/description of 'absent' images) found in fashion magazines.

15. Despite Barthes's 1962 article on Lévi-Strauss, 'Sociology and socio-logic' (Barthes 1987), implicitly linked to Durkheim in the early preface to *The Fashion System*; see also Carter 2003: 152.

16. '"Blue is in Fashion This Year"' displays the earliest version of the semiologist's example of the traffic light, which reappears in *The Fashion System* (1985a: 3.3–3.5, 29–33) and also in *Elements of Semiology* before it.

17. Propp described the 'two-fold quality of a tale' thus: 'Its amazing multiformity, picturesqueness, and colour, and on the other hand, its no less striking uniformity, its repetition' (2000 [1928]: 20–21).

18. I disagree with Moeran (2004: 37) when he suggests that to concentrate on the signifiers of fashion, as Barthes does in *The Fashion System*, is to ignore taste. Surely Barthes's point about written fashion being the only aspect of fashion that has no practical or aesthetic function is a fairly straightforward one: no *worn* fashion item (to my knowledge) actually *displays* its written commentary (though it would be an interesting experiment). In other words, the garment-wearer has no guarantee of fashionable status in the eyes of the Other. And this is precisely what Barthes wanted to underline: namely, that fashion, like literature, cannot survive without a written discourse – albeit found elsewhere, i.e. in fashion magazines for the former and in literary criticism for the latter. The Other who then perceives the worn garment as fashionable is then beholden to current definitions of 'taste', found in written fashion, as if the garment-wearer were 'winking' this written 'guarantee' to them.

19. We must remember that Barthes is writing on class 'distinction' long before Pierre Bourdieu's *magnum opus* on the subject (1984 [1979]); and, interestingly, Bourdieu pays scant regard to fashion in his social critique of judgement and taste, preferring a more statistical analysis of clothing and make-up habits.

20. No one has noted (to my knowledge) the affinity between Barthes's thoughts on clothing and signification to those of Marx in *Capital* vol.1. Barthes's choice of the coat as his example repeats

Marx's discussion of the coat in relation to linen and labour in an uncanny way; see the discussion of the coat in *Capital* vol. 1, (138–163, and especially 143) where Marx states: '[W]ithin its value-relation to linen, the coat signifies more than it does outside it...'. Indeed, Barthes's three choices of object for his semiological studies in the early 1960s – food, clothing and shelter – are distinctly Marxian in their fundamental role within human society.

21. Another would be the idea of the combination. If the 1960s was the decade of parody in fashion terms, where the 'dialectic of fashion' ruled (Lobenthal 1990: 245), then for Barthesian fashion theory this was an excellent example of the dialectic of the 'semelfactive' form (once-only, truly original) versus its repetitive, recycling in different combinations – what Gilles Deleuze called, in good Nietzschean fashion, 'difference and repetition' (1968).

22. The 'Eleatic school', founded around 540 BC at Elea by Xenophanes with Parmenides and Zeno, held to a monist, monotheist materialism, which, using reason rather than the senses, denied plurality and change in the universe.

23. As Lavers (146–47) points out, double articulation was soundly rejected also by semiologists such as Umberto Eco and Christian Metz in their work on the image.

24. Althusser was another structuralist wary of analogical and generalist thought (see Suchting 2004: 39); see also Barthes's own definition (2003: 157).

25. One noteworthy 'solution' to the history/structure, or change/order, debate is to be found in evolutionary biology, where Stephen Jay Gould's notion of 'punctuated equilibrium' allows organisms to mix formal stability with sudden seismic changes in form, across both very long and minutely short periods of time (Jay Gould 2002: especially chapter 9).

26. The shifters that Barthes uses himself – 'voilà' (here), 'voyez' (look) and other shifter commands in his own writing – are underlined by Butor (1974: 380–81). Mallarmé is a key referent for Lecercle (1989: 61 ff.) who notices deep similarities in Barthes's and Mallarmé's use not only of the quote but also of the 'shifter'.

27. Though ready-to-wear manufacture had existed in France for a century, practised by France's Jewish community, it was decimated by the Nazi deportations (Steele 1998: 281).

28. Only for Madsen, a sympathetic biographer of Chanel, to remind us that Courrèges's company was 50 per cent owned by L'Oréal, 'a sign of the times' that Chanel was able to avoid (ibid.).

29. Butor calls Barthes's 1967 piece on Chanel and Courrèges an 'indispensable complement' to *The Fashion System* (396), and he imagines the pleasure for Barthes of being invited into the women's 'citadelle' (ibid.). Butor even considers *The Fashion System* as a pseudo-Ph.D. thesis, because all of the quotes from the various women's magazines are not listed (as is the case in its forerunner, chapter 4 here). Butor also points out that the citations often involve English words, making the whole corpus into a kind of 'foreign' language, redolent no doubt of the influence of British styles in 1960s France.

30. Interestingly it is the Surrealist Pierre Reverdy that Chanel claims is the greatest of poets, and certainly not Cocteau who, she insists, was far from original (Madsen 1990: 301). This is something that Barthes does not mention in his literary roll-call.

31. Indeed, as Calvet argues (1973: 79–80, 96), it was written fashion, or the literature of fashion, which allowed Barthes to move on to literature proper and analyse it semiologically. In fact, in Calvet's view, Barthes had come to a bit of a dead end in the early 1960s, unable to get close to how literature actually works; and it was precisely the decision to work on written, verbalized fashion that would inspire his work on Flaubert in 1967 and then on Balzac in 1968–1969.

32. When Barthes speaks of the 'detail' as a crucial ornament operating on the meaning of an outfit, we must not confuse this with 'ornamentation', one of the three motivational categories that Barthes had discarded in his explanation of clothing. The only point of continuity between pre- and post-1968 in Barthes's work seems to be the 'detail'. The 'detail' becomes pivotal in his move from a rather heady, scientistic structuralism to a more slippery and playful post-structuralism. 'Detail' also becomes, in late 1960s France, an anti-technocratic, 'scandalous' element in critical essayism.

33. At the same time as he is writing 'Towards a Sociology of Dress' and '"Blue is in Fashion This Year"', Barthes was also publishing his piece 'History or Literature?' (1992 [1963]). In it he applied his view (set out also in chapter 1 here) that there is a *non-*

equivalence between clothing and history to the theatre of Racine and to literature in general: for literature too is 'at once a sign of history, and a resistance to this history' (1992: 155).

34. This socially interpretative analysis of fashion forms recurs in Barthes's work right up until his death. The analysis of the Quaker origins of men's aristocratic fashion was useful in the very final 'dossier' of his life, on Nadar's photographic portraits of the people in the world of Proust (2003: 394). Here for Barthes the whole social dialectic of men's clothing revolved around distinction: mon-archical outfits of the leisured classes versus the democratic Quaker clothes adapted for workers.

35. In 1971 Barthes tells Stephen Heath that he is close to Derrida in having 'the feeling of participating (of wanting to participate) in a period of history that Nietzsche calls "nihilism"' (1985b: 133) – a nihilism of which Punk fashion would have been proud.

36. The number of *Communications* in which Barthes's piece on hippies appears is introduced by Edgar Morin's essay which takes 'recuperation' as its key theme in this new post-1968 world: 'We are back to endemic crisis and neo-recuperation', argues Morin (1969: 19), in which 'Cultural negativity (anomia, madness, auto-didacticism, radical critique) becomes itself a positive form. Indeed conformism is obliged to integrate non-conformism… Whether in the form of defusing, spiriting away or integration, recuperation really is a vital process within the cultural system… As soon as there is system there is recuperation' (15). Gaudibert (1971: 114–21) traces the theory of 'recuperation' back to the writings of Benjamin, Pierre Naville and Trotsky.

37. Karl Marx in *Change* 4 (1969: 8), but not quoted from *Change* 2 (82–83) as is claimed. The piece from Marx's *Capital* is 'La métamorphose des marchandises', a section which had not been translated into French from *Capital* vol. 1 (see *Das Kapital*, Berlin, Band/Dietz Verlag, 1957, 109–10). The special number of *Change* on fashion then includes pieces on fashion by Jean Paris, Claude Ollier, Philippe Boyer, Paul Zumthor, Michel Butor, Jean-Paul Aron, with two fragments by Balzac and one by Mallarmé, finishing with Jean-Pierre Faye's piece on Mallarmé and then Eric Clemens's and Barthes's pieces on fashion rhetoric.

38. It is worth remembering also that *Change* is about to go through a rather nasty and bitter public argument with its radical counterpart *Tel Quel*; Faye resigns from *Tel Quel* in disgust, and Barthes defends the latter against *Change*.

39. Though Lemoine-Luccioni (28) quotes (curiously) Hegel, and then Lévi-Strauss's *Mythologiques vol. 4. L'homme nu* (Paris, Plon, 1971), as saying that the nude does *not* signify. For this reason, Luccioni-Lemoine rejects the signifier–signified dichotomy when it makes the body into the signified of fashion, because there is no such thing, she argues following a 'zero-degree' optic, as a nude body (43).

40. Here in 1978, Barthes's emphasis is on how the body has been hidden, suggesting that aristocratic clothes and work clothes signalled the wearer's social class. But with work clothes, he goes on, this led paradoxically to the body being 'exteriorized', 'identified as occupying a particular place in a social hierarchy' (913). Interestingly also, Barthes suggests here in 1978 that the gregariousness of contemporary clothing means that the body is inflected by clothing forms and styles (Barthes's example is hairstyles), to the extent that differences between the sexes in clothing have all but disappeared (914).

## *Editor's Note and Acknowledgements*

I have used the versions of Barthes's pieces on clothing and fashion as they appear in their original place of publication, though the anthology *Le Bleu est à la mode cette année. Et autres articles* (Paris, Institut Français de la Mode, 2001) was invaluable. As well as the original place of publication, the reader will also find a reference to the French version as it appears in Barthes's *Oeuvres complètes* (3 volumes, Paris, Seuil 1993, 1994 and 1995).

There is also in this anthology, I am pleased to say, a piece which was unpublished in Barthes's lifetime, an early version of the preface to *The Fashion System*. This manuscript appeared recently in a special number of the Swiss journal *[VWA]* ('Le Cabinet des manuscrits'), no. 25 (spring) 1998, 7–28); and I am grateful to the editors of this journal as well as to the 'Cabinet des manuscrits' at the Bibliothèque de la Chaux-de-Fonds in Switzerland for permitting me to include it here. Unfortunately there is no date on the manuscript and no recollection of its place of composition. As an early draft of the preface to *The Fashion System* it seems (by my guess) to have been written around 1963. I have translated the footnotes (somewhat incomplete) as they appear in *VWA* whilst trying to supply further information where necessary or possible. This applies in fact to all of Barthes's referencing in this book, especially in footnotes, and any clarifications made are signalled by ['Editors' note']. A glossary of names is also included at the end of the anthology.

Barthes is renowned as a skilful and sometimes startling essayist in the great French tradition (though this expression might surprise his acolytes). The reader will hopefully appreciate then that any rendering into English of Barthes's formulation may sometimes sound awkward. Such an outcome, though traded against precision in the translation, will be entirely my own, and I do not wish to associate with this excess any of the following who helped with this book: Nigel Armstrong, Marie-Claire Barnet, Françoise Coquet, Claude Coste, Sarah Donachie, Jennie Dorny and Les Editions du Seuil in Paris, Stuart Elden, Charles Forsdick, Anne Freadman, Russell Goulbourne, Laurence Grove, Barry Heselwood, Diana Holmes, Roxane Jubert, Peter Keller, Naaman Kessous, Rachel Killick, Diana Knight, Hannah Littlejones, David Musgrave, Julian Pefanis, Barbara Plaschy and the *Landesbibliothek* in Bern, Bruno Remaury, David Roe, Nigel Saint, Michael Sheringham, staff in Special Collections in the Brotherton Library at the University of Leeds, Graham Stafford, David Steel, Caroline Mossy Stride, Patrick Suter, Yves Velan.

Mick Carter has been an unending source of support, guidance and discussion and performed PVC-tight readings of earlier versions of my translations and of the Afterword. Victoria Dawson played a pivotal role at crucial moments in the preparation of this book. Finally, I would like to dedicate this book to my parents; and also to a Celtic ring which decided, one windy afternoon on Bradda Head, to return to its origins.

*Andy Stafford*

# Bibliography

## Works by Roland Barthes

(1953), 'Visages et figures', in *Esprit,* July (repub. in Barthes 1993a).

(1968 [1964]), *Elements of Semiology,* trans. Annette Lavers and Colin Smith, New York: Hill and Wang.

(1970 [1953]), *Writing Degree Zero,* trans. Annette Lavers and Colin Smith, Boston, Mass.: Beacon Press.

(1971), 'Réponses', in *Tel Quel,* 47, 89–107.

(1972 [1964]), *Critical Essays,* Evanston: Northwestern University Press.

(1975 [1970]), *S/Z,* trans. Richard Miller, London: Jonathan Cape.

(1977a [1971]), *Sade, Fourier, Loyola,* trans. Richard Miller, London: Jonathan Cape.

(1977b), *Image, Music, Text,* trans. Stephen Heath, Glasgow: Fontana.

(1979), *The Eiffel Tower and Other Mythologies,* trans. Richard Howard, New York: Hill and Wang.

(1985a [1967]), *The Fashion System,* trans. Matthew Ward and Richard Howard, London: Jonathan Cape.

(1985b), *The Grain of the Voice. Interviews 1962–1980,* trans. Linda Coverdale, New York: Hill and Wang.

(1985c), *The Responsibility of Forms. Critical Essays on Music, Art and Representation,* trans. Richard Howard, Oxford: Blackwell.

(1986), *The Rustle of Language,* trans. Richard Howard, Oxford: Blackwell.

(1987a [1954]), *Michelet,* trans. Richard Howard, Oxford: Blackwell.

(1987b), *The Semiotic Challenge,* trans. Richard Howard, Oxford: Blackwell.

(1992 [1963]), *On Racine*, trans. Richard Howard, Berkeley/Los Angeles: University of California Press.

(1993a), *Oeuvres complètes t.I*, Paris: Seuil.

(1993b [1972/1957]), *Mythologies*, trans. Annette Lavers, London: Vintage.

(1994), *Oeuvres complètes t.II*, Paris: Seuil.

(1995), *Oeuvres complètes t.III*, Paris: Seuil.

(2001), *Le Bleu est à la mode cette année. Et Autres Articles*, Paris: Institut Français de la Mode (IFM).

(2003), *La Préparation du Roman*, Paris: Seuil/IMEC.

Bourdieu, P. (1984 [1979]), *Distinction. A Social Critique of the Judgement of Taste*, London: Routledge and Kegan Paul.

Burgelin, O. (1974), 'Le double système de la mode', in *l'Arc*, 56, 8–16 (republished in Barthes 2001).

Butor, M. (1974), 'La Fascinatrice', in *Répertoire IV*, Paris: Editions de Minuit, 371–97.

Calvet, L.-J. (1973), *Roland Barthes. Un regard politique sur le signe*, Paris: Payot.

—— (1994), *Roland Barthes: A Biography*, trans. Sarah Wykes, Cambridge: Polity Press.

Carter, M. (2003), *Fashion Classics. From Carlyle to Barthes*, Oxford: Berg.

Charles-Roux, E. (1981), *Chanel and her World*, London: Weidenfield & Nicolson.

Culler, J. (1975), *Structuralist Poetics: Structuralism, Linguistics and the Study of Literature*, London: Routledge and Kegan Paul.

Deleuze, G. (1968). *Différence et répétition*, Paris: PUF.

Elden, S. (2003), *Henri Lefebvre*, New York/London: Continuum.

Fortassier, R. (1988), *Les écrivains français et la mode. De Balzac à nos jours*, Paris: Presses Universitaires de France.

Fromm, E. (1979), *To Have or To Be?*, London: Sphere.

Gaudibert, P. (1971), *Action culturelle: intégration et/ou subversion*, Paris: Casterman.

Godfrey, S. (1982), 'The Dandy as Ironic Figure', in *Sub-Stance*, XI: 3, 21–33.

Granger, G.-G. (1968), *Essai d'une philosophie du style*, Paris: Armand Colin.

Greimas, A.J. (2000), *La mode en 1830. Langage et société: écrits de jeunesse*, Paris: Presses Universitaires de France.

Guillaume, V. (1998), *Courrèges*, London: Thames and Hudson.

Haye, A. de la & Tobin, S. (1994), *Chanel. The Couturiére at Work*, London: Victoria and Albert Museum.

Hegel, G. W. F. (1975), *Aesthetics. Lectures on Fine Art*, 2 vols, trans. T. M. Knox, Oxford: Clarendon Press.

Hobsbawm, E. (2002), *Interesting Times: A Twentieth Century Life*, London: Allen Lane.

Jakobson, R. (1963), *Essais de linguistique générale*, Paris: Seuil.

—— (1990), *On Language*, eds L. Waugh & M. Monville-Burston, Cambridge, Mass./London: Harvard University Press.

Jay Gould, S. (2002), *The Structure of Evolutionary Theory*, Cambridge, Mass.: Harvard University Press.

Jobling, P. (1999), *Fashion Spreads. Word and Image in Fashion Photography Since 1980*, Oxford/New York: Berg.

Kelly, M. (2000), 'Demystification: A Dialogue between Barthes and Lefebvre', in *Yale French Studies*, 98, 79–97.

Kempf, R. (1977), *Dandies. Baudelaire et cie*, Paris: Seuil.

Klopp, G. (ed.) (1991), *Mille ans de costume français, 950-1950*, Thionville: Gérard Klopp.

Knight, D. (1997), *Barthes and Utopia. Space, Travel, Writing*, Oxford: Oxford University Press.

Kohan, N. (2005), 'Postmodernism, commodity fetishism and hegemony', in *International Socialism Journal*, 105 (Winter), 139-158.

La Croix, A. de (1987), *Roland Barthes. Pour une éthique des signes*, Brussels: De Boeck-Wesmael.

Lane, M. ed., (1970), *Structuralism. A Reader*, London: Jonathan Cape.

Laver, J. (1968), *Dandies*, London: Weidenfeld and Nicolson.

Lavers, A. (1982), *Roland Barthes: Structuralism and After*, London: Methuen.

Lecercle, J.-P. (1989), *Mallarmé et la mode*, Paris: Séguier.

Lefebvre, H. (1966), *Le langage et la société*, Paris: Gallimard.

—— (1975), *L'idéologie structuraliste*, Paris: Anthropos.

—— (2003), *Key Writings*, eds S. Elden, E. Lebas & E. Kofman, New York/London: Continuum.

Lemoine-Luccioni, E. (1983), *La robe. Essai psychanalytique sur le vêtement, suivi d'un entretien avec André Courrèges*, Paris: Seuil.

Lipovetsky, G. (1994 [1987]), *The Empire of Fashion, Dressing Modern Democracy*, trans. Catherine Porter, Princeton, New Jersey: Princeton University Press.

Lobenthal, J. (1990), *Radical Rags. Fashions of the Sixties*, New York: Abbeville Press.

Lurie, A. (1992 [1981]), *The Language of Clothes*, London: Bloomsbury.

Madsen, A. (1990), *Coco Chanel. A Biography*, London: Bloomsbury.

Mallarmé, S. (2004 [1874]), *Mallarmé on Fashion* (*La Dernière Mode*, ed. and trans. by P. Furbank and A. Cain), Oxford: Berg.

Marly, D. de (1986), *Working Dress. A History of Occupational Clothing*, London: Batsford Press.

Marx, K. (1986 [1867]), *Capital vol. 1*, Harmondsworth: Penguin.

Melly, G. (1971 [1970]), *Revolt into Style. The Pop Arts*, New York: Anchor Books.

Moeran, B. (2004), 'A Japanese Discourse of Fashion and Taste', in *Fashion Theory* 8:1 (March), 35–62.

Moriarty, M. (1991), *Roland Barthes*, Oxford: Polity.

Morin, M. (1969), 'De la culturanalyse à la politique culturelle' in *Communications* 14, 1969, 5–38.

Mullan, J. (2002), 'Nothing Quite Adds Up', in *The Guardian*, G2, 4 October, 8.

Nairn, T. (1967), 'Fashionable Structures', in *The New Statesman*, 11 August, 174.

Perrot, P. (1981 [1994]), *Fashioning the Bourgeoisie. A History of Clothing in the Nineteenth Century*, trans. R. Bienvenu, Princeton, New Jersey: Princeton University Press.

Propp, V. (2000 [1928]), *Morphology of the Folktale*, Austin: University of Texas.

Rylance, R. (1994), *Roland Barthes*, Hemel Hempstead: Harvester Wheatsheaf.

Sheringham, M. (2000), 'Fashion, Theory and the Everyday: Barthes, Baudrillard, Lipovetsky, Maffesoli', in *Dalhousie French Studies*, 53 (Winter), 144–54.

—— (2005), *Everyday Life: Theories and Practices from Surrealism to the Present*, Oxford: Oxford University Press.

Sontag, S. (ed.) (1982), *A Barthes Reader*, New York: Hill & Wang.

Stafford, A. (1998), *Roland Barthes, Phenomenon and Myth. An Intellectual Biography*, Edinburgh: Edinburgh University Press.

Steele, V. (1998 [1988]), *Paris Fashion. A Cultural History*, Oxford/New York: Berg.

Stern, R. (2004), *Against Fashion. Clothing as Art, 1850–1930*, Cambridge, Mass.: MIT Press.

Suchting, W. (2004), 'Althusser's Late Thinking about Materialism', in *Historical Materialism*, 12: 1, 3–70.

Temple, M. (1999), '*On s'est tous défilé* de Jean-Luc Godard (1988)', in *La Chouette* 30, 83–87.

Thienen, F. van (1961), *Huit siècles de costume. Histoire de la Mode en Occident*, Verviers: Editions Gérard et Co.

Todorov, T. (1965), *Théorie de la littérature. Ecrits des formalistes russes*, Paris: Seuil.

Vincent-Ricard, F. (1987), *La Mode*, Paris: Seghers.

White, N. and Griffiths, I. (2000), *The Fashion Business. Theory, Practice, Image*, Oxford: Berg.

Whitley, J. (1969), 'Interview with Roland Barthes', in *The Sunday Times*, 2 February, 55.

# Glossary of Names

**Giuseppe Arcimboldo** (1527–1593) Milan-born Italian painter, famous for his garish portraits showing heads made of fruit and vegetables.

**Honoré de Balzac** (1799–1850) Major French novelist and short-story writer, author of the *Comédie humaine*, a realist cycle of novels on human society renowned for their social and individual descriptions. Also a hack and journalist, this keen observer of humans wrote anonymous *physiologies*, some of which covered fashion and clothing. Barthes's 1970 essay *S/Z* was an avant-garde reading of one of Balzac's more gothic short stories, *Sarrasine*.

**Jules Barbey d'Aurévilly** (1808–1889) French novelist and journalist, a right-wing and anti-democratic dandy, whose sadistic and transgressive writings were in contrast to his Catholicism. Wrote an important essay on dandyism and Beau Brummell (*Complete Works* vol II).

**Charles Baudelaire** (1821–1867) Notorious French romantic poet and art critic, who wrote on the dandy, on women and their clothing, and on make-up.

**Fernand Braudel** (1902-1985) French historian of the *Annales* school, who wrote on the Mediterranean and on the emergence of capitalism using the *longue durée* theory inspired by Lucien Febvre and Marc Bloch, and also wrote on material culture.

**Thomas Carlyle** (1795–1881) British historian, essayist and novelist, famous in fashion studies for his curious novel *Sartor Resartus. The Life and Opinions of Herr Teufelsdröckh* (1841).

**Gabrielle 'Coco' Chanel** (1883–1971) World-famous French clothes and fashion designer, renowned for her classic and traditional styles for women, who worked with Cocteau, Diaghilev and

Stravinsky, and was a friend of Paul Morand. Compromised by her relations with the Nazi occupiers of France during the Second World War, Chanel returned to fashion fame after the war, and resumed her Parisian lifestyle.

**Jean Cocteau** (1889–1963) Avant-garde French poet, novelist, playwright, film-maker, painter and illustrator, who drew for Chanel and wrote on fashion: what he called this 'stunning epidemic'. See the recent number of *Cahiers Jean Cocteau* (no. 3, 2004), on Cocteau and fashion.

**André Courrèges** (1923–) French fashion designer who began his career at Balenciaga and then in 1961 set up his own fashion house, where he produced radically new fashions including angular dresses and trouser suits, especially renowned for his 'space-age' outfits. 'Discovered' the miniskirt at the same time as Mary Quant; he also wanted to make fashionable clothing affordable.

**Jacques Damourette** (1873–1943) French grammarian and author, with Edouard Pignon, of the *Essai de grammaire de la langue française* (1911–1927), a ground-breaking study of how the French language works.

**Ernest Dichter** (1907–1991) Austrian-American specialist on 'motivation research' and pioneering management consultant; follower of Freud and inventor of the 'focus group'; author of *The Strategy of Desire* (London: T. V. Boardman & Co, 1960).

**Emile Durkheim** (1858–1915) Pioneering French sociologist who believed that humans cannot be reduced to the sum of their psychologies, rather that it is society that defines the human.

**Jean Duvignaud** (1921–) French sociologist and anthropologist, influenced by Durkheim, Marx and Gurvitch, whose work tends to underline the radical and theatrical aspects of human actions.

**Lucien Febvre** (1878–1956) Influential French social historian, colleague of Henri Berr on the inter-war journal *Revue de synthèse historique*, and then founder with Marc Bloch of the *Annales* school; played an important role in setting up the VIth section of the Ecole Pratique des Hautes Etudes (EPHE) in Paris where Barthes began to research in 1960. Febvre's work was renowned for its blending of geography and psychology into what he called 'faits de sensibilité'; see his 'Sensibility and History, How to Reconstitute the Emotional Life of the Past', in Febvre, *A New Kind of History and Other Essays* (ed. Peter Burke, trans. K. Folca, New York: Harper and Row, 1973, 12–26).

**André Félibien, sieur des Avaux et de Javercy** (1619–1695) French theorist and writer, historiographer at the Académie Royale, friend and biographer of the painter Poussin. Best known for his *Conversations on the Lives and Work of Ancient and Modern Painters* (1666–1688).

**John Carl Flügel** (1884–1955) British psychologist and psycho-analyst who worked on morals in society and whose *Psychology of Clothes* (1930) is a classic description of human motivations in clothing.

**Charles Fourier** (1772–1837) French Utopian socialist.

**Georges Friedmann** (1902–1977) French sociologist and Com-munist Party fellow-traveller; founder (with Georges Gurvitch) of the *Centre d'études sociologiques*, specializing in work-related studies. Employed Barthes and Edgar Morin in 1955 to research work clothing.

**Jean-Claude Gardin** (1925–) French archaeologist and specialist on prehistoric societies at the VIth section of the EPHE, known for his use of semantic studies of ancient pottery, of Bronze Age tools and money; see his *Le fichier mécanographique de l'outillage* (Beyrouth: IFA, 1956), and 'Four Codes for the Description of Artefacts: An Essay in Anthropological Technique and Theory', *American Anthropologist* (60:2, 1958).

**Marcel Granet** (1884–1940) Influential French sinologist, see his *La Civilization chinoise*, (Paris: Club du livre de l'histoire, 1958 [1929], trans. as *Chinese Civilization*, by Kathleen Innes and Mable Brailsford, London: Keegan Paul, 1930); or his *Etudes sociologiques sur la Chine* (Paris: PUF, 1953).

**Gilles-Gaston Granger** (1920–) Epistemologist and philosopher of science, professor at the Collège de France, major influence on Michel Foucault, though less historically relativist than the latter and more Kuhnian in his understanding of theoretical and scientific 'ruptures' and continuities; see his *Pensée formelle et sciences de l'homme* (Paris: Aubier, 1960).

**Algirdas Julien Greimas** (1917–1992) Lithuanian-born French linguist and specialist in semantics at the EPHE. Having written his doctorate on fashion language in 1947, he became friends with Barthes in Egypt and introduced him to Saussure's work, and became a pioneer in the 1960s of semiotics and structuralist analysis of discourse.

**Paul Guillaume** (1878–1962) French 'gestaltist' psychologist, who followed the German Gestalt tradition of seeing mental phenomena as 'extended' events, and the cognitive process as one which changes the perceiver's perceptive field forever.

**Georges Gurvitch** (1894–1965) Important French sociologist, colleague of Georges Friedmann and specialist on Marcel Mauss and the dialectics of totality; see his *Dialectique et sociologie* (Paris: Flammarion, 1962) and *The Social Frameworks of Knowledge* (trans. Margaret and Kenneth Thompson, Oxford: Blackwell, 1971).

**Georg W. F. Hegel** (1770–1831) German romantic philosopher; wrote briefly but influentially on clothing, in *Aesthetics* vols. I and II.

**Louis Hjelmslev** (1899–1965) Danish linguist influenced by Saussure who set out the three levels of *langue* as 'schema', 'norm' and 'usage', and proposed that a sign was not only denotative but also connotative.

**Roman Jakobson** (1896–1982) Russian-born linguist and phonologist of the Prague Circle, Jakobson was a formalist, early structuralist and literary critic, whose work on metaphor and metonymy influenced Claude Lévi-Strauss.

**Elihu Katz** (1926–) American sociologist and specialist on media and communication; worked with Paul Lazarsfeld.

**Alfred Kroeber** (1876–1960) American anthropologist, specialist on Native Americans who also wrote on cycles in social history, in particular in relation to fashion.

**Jacques Lacan** (1901–1981) French psychiatrist and psychoanalyst whose work has informed post-structuralism. Believing that the unconscious is structured like a language, and applying Saussure's theories of language to Freudianism, Lacanian theory tended to be suspicious of attempts to tie the signified too tightly to the signifier.

**Jean Laplanche** (1924–) French psychoanalyst and translator, with Jean-Baptiste Pontalis, of Freud's writings into French; also worked with Serge Leclaire on Lacanian theories.

**Valery Larbaud** (1881–1957) French novelist, poet, essayist and translator, whose wealth and cosmopolitanism made him an important inter-war literary figure.

**Nicolas de Larmessin** (1632–1694) French illustrator, one of a family of engravers working in the 'Pomme d'Or' in Rue St Jacques in Paris, whose work centred on grotesque images of trades people dressed in the objects and tools appropriate to their profession.

**François (Duc de) La Rochefoucauld** (1613–1680) French 'moralist' writer; famously wrote maxims pithy in style and philosophical in content, and best known for his thoughts on *amour propre* and *honnêteté*.

**Paul Lazarsfeld** (1901–1976) American sociologist famous for his studies of lifestyle choice and of voting tendencies.

**Serge Leclaire** (1924–1994) Neuro-psychiatrist and psychoanalyst, co-founder (with Jacques Lacan) of the *Société Française de Psychanalyse*, worked with Jean Laplanche on Lacanian concepts.

**Henri Lefebvre** (1905–1991) French Marxist philosopher, famous for his *Critique of Everyday Life*, and for work on cities and on Marxist philosophy.

**André Leroi-Gourhan** (1911–1986) French archaeologist and ethnologist of prehistoric times, renowned for his study of human tools and prehistoric material culture.

**Claude Lévi-Strauss** (1908–) Major French anthropologist of the structuralist-functionalist school, whose work on totemism and kinship, on myth and social structure, was an important influence on Barthes.

**Stéphane Mallarmé** (1842–1898) French symbolist poet whose writing epitomizes the self-absorbed literary imagination of French literature. Both difficult and musical, his writings in prose and poetry are concerned often with blankness, nothingness and emptiness. He also wrote a fashion magazine, written under various pseudonyms and aimed entirely at himself, called *La Dernière Mode*, for which see *Mallarmé on Fashion* (Oxford: Berg, 2004).

**Pierre Marivaux** (1688–1763) French playwright, novelist and essayist, best-known for his comedies depicting characters coming to terms with love and social mores.

**André Martinet** (1908–) French linguist and major advocate of Saussure's functionalist view of language, who emphasized the communicative aspect and the effects of speaker's choices.

**Jules Michelet** (1798–1874) The most famous of France's Romantic historians, championed by Febvre and Braudel for his ideal of a 'total' history and for his insights into hitherto marginalized aspects of social history such as sex, nutrition and natural science. Barthes wrote his second book on this most unorthodox of patriotic historians, selecting extracts from Michelet's monumental works and then illustrating and commenting upon them (1954). Like Balzac, Michelet was fond of description, including that of clothing.

**Paul Morand** (1888–1976) Diplomat and travel writer, dashing member of Parisian high society and friend of Coco Chanel, compromised by serving as a Vichy ambassador in Romania and Switzerland during the Second World War.

**Georges Mounin** (1910–) Important, if somewhat overlooked, French linguist, who worked alongside André Martinet and promoted the 'double articulation' theory of communication.

**Alfred de Musset** (1810–1857) French Romantic poet, dramatist and novelist, elected to the Académie Française in 1852, famous also for his amorous links to Georges Sand and for his head of long hair.

**Friedrich Nietzsche** (1844–1900) German philosopher of power, 'super-humans' and nihilism.

**Blaise Pascal** (1623–1662) French mathematician, scientist and literary stylist, famous for his posthumously published collection of laconic and terse thoughts on life, death and religion, the *Pensées*, which combine Christian apologetics, including theories of original sin, with metaphysical speculation.

**Edouard Pichon** (1890–1940) French linguist working alongside Jacques Damourette (see above), and a psychologist of language specializing in tenses.

**Edgar Allan Poe** (1809–1849) American poet, critic and short-story writer, renowned for his gothic stories and interest in horror, translated into French by Charles Baudelaire.

**Paul Poiret** (1879–1944) Parisian fashion designer who, around 1908, removed all types of ornament from women's clothing, replacing this with lively colours in the materials chosen. Followed by many at the time, but after the First World War illness and financial difficulties ended his period of glory; memoirs published as *En habillant l'époque* (Paris: Bernard Grasset, 1986).

**Marcel Proust** (1871–1922) France's greatest novelist of the twentieth century, thanks to his nine-volume novel *A la recherche du temps* *perdu.* Influenced by Balzac, the novel deals as much with memory as it does with painting the aristocratic society of *belle époque* France, including the fashions and clothes of the time.

**Jean Racine** (1639–1699) French classical dramatist, one of France's most celebrated writers, on whose plays Barthes published a polemical, structuralist study, *On Racine,* in 1963.

**Henri Raymond** (1921–) French sociologist and urban geographer.

**Marthe Robert** (1914–1996) French essayist and Germanist, who wrote on Freud, Kafka, Nietzsche and Dostoevsky.

**Jean-Paul Sartre** (1905–1980) Important French philosopher, novelist and dramatist, famous for his political *engagement* and defence of existentialism; the latter was used to describe and immortalize Jean Genet, the poet and thief, as a kind of martyr of radical social action.

**Ferdinand de Saussure** (1857–1913) Swiss linguist and father of semiology whose published lecture notes, *Cours de linguistique générale* (1916), have had enormous influence on French literature, literary and cultural criticism, social science and philosophy. His main innovation was to consider language and meaning as synchronic (rather than diachronic, or purely etymological). Made up of a signifier and a signified, which are linked in an arbitrary (unmotivated) way, the sign is at the heart of language; humans communicate by choosing from a stock of words and syntactic rules (*langue*) which they use and combine with other words and rules to form speech acts (*parole*). Barthes used Saussure's distinctions to forward his analysis of clothing and fashion forms, transposing the semiological distinctions in the Saussurian account of language and its operations to the world of clothing.

**Marie ('Madame') de Sévigné** (1626–1696) One of the most influential female French writers, famous for her literary and socially minded correspondence. Controversial and contemporary, this collection of letters is a window both on to private life and courtly society.

**Herbert Spencer** (1820–1903) British sociologist who believed that life was governed by laws and that these laws could be used to set up a theory of social evolution.

**Jean Stoetzel** (1910–1987) French sociologist and director of the *Revue française de sociologie*, whose work specialized in public opinion, religion and social psychology.

**Knud Togeby** (1918–1974) Danish linguist of the Copenhagen circle and scholar of the saga, specializing in tenses; his study of the French language, *Structure immanente de la langue française* (Nordisk Sprog og Kulturforlag, 1951), was influential at the time.

**Nikolai Sergeevich Trubetskoy** (1890–1938) Russian phonologist and morphologist, translated by Roman Jakobson.

**Wilhelm Max Wundt** (1832–1920) Early German psychologist, of the voluntarist school, who put forward the idea of humans' 'heterogony of ends' which suggested that an individual does not have tunnel vision when pursuing a goal, and therefore is highly unpredictable.

**Emile Zola** (1840–1902) Influential French novelist and critic, famous also for his stance in favour of the falsely accused Jewish (traitor) of France, Alfred Dreyfus. His novels are renowned for their naturalist, reform-minded portrayal of social conditions in late nineteenth-century France, in which poverty, alienation and commodity fetishism feature as fundamental human ills; his 1883 novel *Au bonheur des dames* looked at the effect of the department store display – especially fashion – on popular consciousness.

# Index